Printed in the United States
By Bookmasters

Psychological Insights for Understanding COVID-19 and Work

In the *Psychological Insights for Understanding COVID-19* series, international experts introduce important themes in psychological science that engage with people's unprecedented experience of the pandemic, drawing together chapters as they originally appeared before COVID-19 descended on the world.

This timely and accessible book brings together a selection of chapters offering insights into issues surrounding work and the COVID-19 pandemic. Featuring content on topics such as health and wellbeing, work-family, flexible hours, organisational communication, talent management, recovery from work, employee engagement and flourishing, burnout and organisational interventions, the book includes a specially written introduction contextualising the chapters in relation to the COVID-19 crisis. Reflecting on how psychological research is relevant during a significant global event, the introduction examines the potential future impact of the pandemic on the practice and study of psychology and our lives more generally.

Featuring theory and research on key topics germane to the global pandemic, the *Psychological Insights for Understanding COVID-19* series offers thought-provoking reading for professionals, students, academics and policy makers concerned with the psychological consequences of COVID-19 for individuals, families and society.

Sir Cary L. Cooper is the 50th Anniversary Professor of Organizational Psychology and Health at the ALLIANCE Manchester Business School, University of Manchester, UK, President of the CIPD and Co-Chair of the National Forum for Health and Wellbeing at Work.

Psychological Insights for Understanding COVID-19

The *Psychological Insights for Understanding COVID-19* series aims to highlight important themes in psychological science that engage with people's unprecedented experience of the COVID-19 pandemic. These short, accessible volumes draw together chapters as they originally appeared before COVID-19 descended on the world but demonstrate how researchers and professionals in psychological science had developed theory and research on key topics germane to the global pandemic. Each volume includes a specially commissioned, expert introduction that contextualises the chapters in relation to the crisis, reflects on the relevance of psychological research during this significant global event, and proposes future research and vital interventions that elucidate understanding and coping with COVID-19. With individual volumes exploring society, health, family, work and media, the *Psychological Insights for Understanding COVID-19* series offers thought-provoking reading for professionals, students, academics and policy makers concerned with psychological consequences of the pandemic for individuals, families and society.

Titles in the series:

Psychological Insights for Understanding COVID-19 and Families, Parents, and Children
Edited by Marc H. Bornstein

Psychological Insights for Understanding COVID-19 and Media and Technology
Edited by Ciarán Mc Mahon

Psychological Insights for Understanding COVID-19 and Society
Edited by S. Alexander Haslam

Psychological Insights for Understanding COVID-19 and Work
Edited by Cary L. Cooper

Psychological Insights for Understanding COVID-19 and Health
Edited by Dominika Kwasnicka and Robbert Sanderman

For more information about this series, please visit: https://www.routledge.com/ Psychological-Insights-for-Understanding-COVID-19/book-series/COVID

Psychological Insights for Understanding COVID-19 and Work

Edited by Cary L. Cooper

LONDON AND NEW YORK

First published 2021
by Routledge
2 Park Square, Milton Park, Abingdon, Oxon OX14 4RN

and by Routledge
52 Vanderbilt Avenue, New York, NY 10017

Routledge is an imprint of the Taylor & Francis Group, an informa business

British Library Cataloguing-in-Publication Data
A catalogue record for this book is available from the British Library

Library of Congress Cataloging-in-Publication Data
A catalog record for this book has been requested

ISBN: 978-0-367-63609-8 (hbk)
ISBN: 978-0-367-63607-4 (pbk)
ISBN: 978-1-003-11995-1 (ebk)

Typeset in Times New Roman
by Apex CoVantage, LLC

Selected chapters are taken from the following original Routledge publications

Flexible Work: Designing our Healthier Future Lives
Edited by Sarah H. Norgate and Cary L. Cooper
ISBN: 978-0-367-34566-2 (pbk) ISBN: 978-0-429-32658-5 (ebk)

Managing Health and Wellbeing in the Public Sector: A Guide to Best Practice
Ian Hesketh and Cary L. Cooper
ISBN: 978-1-138-92920-3 (pbk) ISBN: 978-1-315-68134-4 (ebk)

From Talent Management to Talent Liberation: A Practical Guide for Professionals, Managers and Leaders
Maggi Evans, John Arnold, and Andrew Rothwell
ISBN: 978-0-367-23298-6 (pbk) ISBN: 978-0-429-27920-1 (ebk)

Positive Psychological Science: Improving Everyday Life, Well-Being, Work, Education, and Societies Across the Globe
Edited by Stewart I. Donaldson, Mihaly Csikszentmihalyi, and Jeanne Nakamura
ISBN: 978-1-138-30229-7 (pbk) ISBN: 978-0-203-73183-3 (ebk)

The Work-Family Interface in Global Context
Edited by Karen Korabik, Zeynep Aycan, and Roya Ayman
ISBN: 978-1-138-84158-1 (pbk) ISBN: 978-1-315-73208-4 (ebk)

Managing for Resilience: A Practical Guide for Employee Wellbeing and Organizational Performance
Edited by Monique F. Crane
ISBN: 978-1-138-12464-6 (pbk) ISBN: 978-1-315-64803-3 (ebk)

Employee Engagement Through Effective Performance Management: A Practical Guide for Managers, Second Edition
Edward M. Mone and Manuel London
ISBN: 978-1-138-64828-9 (pbk) ISBN: 978-1-315-62652-9 (ebk)

Organizational Interventions for Health and Well-being: A Handbook for Evidence-Based Practice
Edited by Karina Nielsen and Andrew Noblet
ISBN: 978-1-138-22142-0 (pbk) ISBN: 978-1-315-41049-4 (ebk)

Contents

Contributors

John Arnold, Loughborough University, UK

Jeff Bednar, Brigham Young University, USA

Cary L. Cooper, University of Manchester, UK

Monique F. Crane, Macquarie University, Australia

Anat Drach-Zahavy, University of Haifa, Israel

Jane E. Dutton, University of Michigan, USA

Maggi Evans, Mosaic Consulting, UK

Henna Hasson, Karolinska Institutet, Sweden

Ian Hesketh, Lancaster University, UK

Manuel London, State University of New York at Stony Brook, USA

Frances McMurtie, Registered Psychologist, Australia

Nicola J. Millard, British Telecommunications, UK

Edward M. Mone, State University of New York at Stony Brook, USA

Anne Richter, Karolinska Institutet, Sweden

Laura Morgan Roberts, University of Virginia, USA

Andrew Rothwell, Loughborough University, UK

Anit Somech, University of Haifa, Israel

Ulrica von Thiele Schwarz, Mälardalen University, Sweden

Introduction

We are going through a period of unprecedented times, during the worst health crisis in the living memories of most of us. This has affected not only our physical and mental wellbeing but also our financial wellbeing, our jobs and employment prospects and the worst economic recession since the Great Depression of the 1930s! And the psychological and economic consequences for individuals and their families are enormous. President Franklin Delano Roosevelt wrote during the Great Depression:

> True individual freedom cannot exist without economic security and independence. People who are hungry and out of a job are the stuff of which dictatorships are made. The hopes of the Republic cannot forever tolerate either undeserved poverty or self-serving wealth.

After the Depression of the 1930s, the recession of the 1980s and the Great Recession of 2008–12, the impact on the individual worker's health and wellbeing as well as on the workplace itself was dramatic and long lasting. The same is happening now as a result of COVID-19 and the subsequent Great Recession/Depression. The workplace is changing in ways we would never have imagined pre-COVID, with many people working substantially from home, with the central office environment a back-up for home working in the service based sectors, with workers' sense of job security gone, with managers' social skills now in greater demand as they manage people more remotely, with email and social platforms in great use as we rely on technology more than ever before, with greater use of robotics and AI in a much more agile workforce, with much more focus on talent management linked to performance at work, with great work-life conflict and greater levels of presenteeism, leavism and stress at work (Hesketh & Cooper, 2019).

During the COVID-19 crisis in May, the UK government's Office of National Statistics did a large-scale national survey (ONS, 2020) on working people. They found that 40% said the coronavirus was adversely affecting their work, and the most common cause was homeworking difficulties. Although some workers had worked flexibly before the lockdown, very few worked exclusively remotely, so getting used to working with family around and children being 'home schooled' was having a negative effect; indeed, 25% of adult workers said that home schooling was 'putting a strain on their relationship'. Also working from home had a negative impact on the health and safety issues of homeworking among one in ten adults, things like not having an appropriate office or office furniture, troubles with computers and printers, etc. There were also major financial concerns, with 23% saying the coronavirus was adversely affecting their household finances, particularly reduced income (70%) and using their personal savings to cover living costs (30%). But by far the worst consequences of coronavirus lockdown and health worries were to do with wellbeing issues, with 48% saying their wellbeing was adversely affected, 75% worried about their jobs in the future, 63% were anxious, 30% felt lonely and 31% felt this period was making their mental health worse.

What COVID-19 did to many, from a psychological perspective, was to create two conditions associated with lack of mental wellbeing: uncertainty and lack of control over the situation. The uncertainty in terms of health, whether they would have a job at the end of the pandemic, will they be able to cope financially, will their skills be needed in the post-COVID-19 era, what will the workplace be like post COVID-19, will technology (eg artificial intelligence, robots) take over their jobs, etc. And then, what control do I have over these? The answer for many was, I have no control over these. But the irony is that actually in many cases you have more control than you think you have, for example, to upskill, or learn more about new technology, or plan your finances better, or ensure you take precautions against the virus on the way to work and in the office, to learn to work more flexibly, etc. As George Bernard Shaw wrote in his play "Mrs. Warren's Profession":

> People are always blaming their circumstances for what they are. I don't believe in circumstances. The people who get on in this world are the people who get up and look for the circumstances they want, and if they can't find them, make them!

Psychological contributions to the impact of COVID-19 on the workplace

It was felt that the issues raised about the impact of COVID-19 have been addressed over the last couple of years in occupational psychology, and that the field would benefit from various outstanding chapters brought together from different books exploring a range of relevant topics raised by the pandemic. We have selected eight chapters from different books which help us put into psychological perspective COVID-19 as it relates to issues in the workplace psychology field. The issues of flexible working, of the use of technology in the future as people work more remotely and flexibly, creating wellbeing cultures in the workplace to reduce stress and improve productivity, how we retain and manage our talent and create prosocial practices, how we reduce work-life conflict and encourage work-life integration, how we enhance individual and organisational resilience and reduce employee burnout in this new world of work and how we design, implement and evaluate intervention programmes in the fast-moving post-COVID-19 world of work.

The first chapter by Nicola J. Millard explores the issues associated with working from home and being totally linked to the digital world. As we enter the post-COVID world of work, people will be working increasingly from home, using the office for an occasional meeting or team building. Communications between people will become more virtual, through emails and communication channels (eg Zoom, Skype, etc.). And given that we will not be seeing our colleagues as much as we did in the past in a central office environment, what we say to people and how we say it becomes even more critical. In addition, she explores the difficulties of switching off in a world dominated by digital devices. Indeed, in France they now have a 'right to disconnect' law, where employers are constrained from sending emails to their staff out of office hours (eg at night, at weekends and while on holiday). So work-life integration is now here, and COVID-19 lockdown in many countries has been the stimulus to what was about to happen in any case, but we still have much to learn.

The second chapter is by Ian Hesketh and Cary L. Cooper and explores what it means in this changing world to create a wellbeing culture in the workplace. With the 'new normal' so different, what are the ingredients of organisational wellbeing? They explore the fundamental tenets of personal resilience, the right environment and aligning leaders to this. This involves doing wellbeing audits, ensuring that from shop floor to top floor there are emotionally literate line managers and creating a culture where employees feel they are valued and trusted at work. As Studs Terkel wrote in his acclaimed book *Working*: "Work is about a search for daily meaning as well as daily bread, for recognition as well as cash, for astonishment rather than torpor, in short, for a sort of life rather than a Monday through Friday sort of dying". Establishing a wellbeing culture in the workplace may not be easy but if you want to retain and attract talent, reduce stress-related illness and get higher productivity this is the way to do it.

The third chapter by Maggi Evans, John Arnold and Andrew Rothwell explores the changing nature of work in the future. Most of these predictions have come true in the post-COVID world. They highlight macro-structures and emerging business models; internal organisational models including the move toward agile, project-based work; demographic changes and global resourcing of talent; technological change toward AI and robotics; and changes in career expectations such as the career experience and discontinuous careers. In the post-COVID world of less secure jobs, higher mobility between jobs, the weakening of the psychological contract at work and the millennials need to be valued and trusted at work, the ability to retain and attract talent will be problematic in the future. Unless we have a new kind of line manager who understands what employees need and supports them to achieve this, talent will disappear. Mark Twain got it right when he said about people in general: "Keep away from people who try to belittle your ambitions. Small people always do that, but the really great make you feel that you, too, can somehow become great".

Chapter 4 by Jane E. Dutton, Laura Morgan Roberts and Jeff Bednar highlights what makes an individual flourish at work given changing circumstances whether it is about technological or economic or organisational change. They explore how the organisation can create a culture that enables employees to flourish at work, where they have a feeling of engagement, motivation, personal growth and self-development. How do organisations enable people to work more flexibly, so that they can get better work-life integration? The focus for the authors is the individual employee and how a positive identity can be created at work that enables them to flourish in their work and life more generally. During COVID-19 many employers focussed on their employees' health and wellbeing as they worked remotely and felt isolated, lonely and worried about their job security. This chapter will help the reader understand as we move into a recession that this 'prosocial' approach can help employees cope with stresses and strains they are likely to experience to reduce ill health and enhance productivity.

The fifth chapter by Anit Somech and Anat Drach-Zahavy explores how a personal coping strategy can help in decreasing the stress of work and family conflict. As we have seen during the COVID-19 lockdown in many countries, the tensions within the family and particularly between partners and spouses have been extraordinarily high as the multiple demands of working from home, home schooling and doing domestic chores have created excessive pressures on relationships. In the future, more and more people will be working substantially from home because the technology enables this plus the employer will try to save money by downsizing office space in expensive urban settings as we enter the recession. So, finding a way to defuse the work and family conflict will be an important strategy not only to help the individual cope with these challenges but also for the employer to get the most out of the employee. The authors provide a roadmap for the individual to cope with 'work interfering with family life' and 'family interference with work' in this ever-changing world, whether it is a result of remote working or not. In life we need a good balance between our family and personal life; work should not predominate to the extent it damages our relationships and ultimately our performance at work as well. As Woody Allen once quipped, "I don't want to achieve immortality through my work, I want to achieve it by not dying!"

Moving on from how people can cope with the 'new normal' at work, Frances McMurtie and Monique F. Crane look at 'the factors that contribute to effective recovery from work, and the practical steps employers and employees can take to maximise the effectiveness of rest periods experienced by employees'. For example, they have found that employees who are encouraged to take up work-related learning and personal development opportunities tend to report higher levels of recovery and relaxation. The pressures that many people will experience over the next couple of years, as we recover from COVID-19 in the midst of a recession, will mean that individuals will need to learn how to rest and psychologically detach from work and engage in the family, take exercise, learn new things and be active in other areas of life. If we can do this, it will positively affect our relationships at work and our productivity at work as well. Leonardo da Vinci once wrote, "Every now and then go away and have a little relaxation. To remain constantly at work will diminish your judgement. Go some distance away, because work will be in perspective and a lack of harmony is more readily seen". As the authors conclude, "the combination of enjoyable work and enjoyable non-work activities is positively associated with high quality recovery".

Following on from exploring getting people to ensure that they rest and recover from the pressures of work when returning after COVID-19 and coping with the recession, we need to manage and prevent employee burnout. Remember from the ONS survey 48% of people during COVID-19 suffered from lack of mental wellbeing, so ensuring that employees don't burn out, as they work longer and unsocial hours to show commitment and presenteeism in the post-COVID era (Cooper & Lu, 2018), Edward M. Mone and Manuel London explore how to recognise the signs of burnout and to create 'greater engagement' and building a climate of trust, empowerment and fairness at work. They emphasise that managers need to help employees learn how to detach appropriately, become more conscious that they are going beyond their 'pressure limits' and feel valued and trusted. As John Ruskin wrote in 1851 at the beginning of the Industrial Revolution "in order that people may be happy in their work, these three things are needed: they must be fit for it; they must not too much of it; and they must have a sense of success in it". If we want to get the best out of people during changing times, it is important to ensure that people can recover and recuperate from the excessive pressures of the workplace.

And finally, given there will be many workplace changes post COVID-19, and as we enter the recession, employers will need to know what works and what doesn't. The chapter by Ulrica von Thiele Schwartz, Anne Richter and Henna Hasson have developed a method of designing, implementing and evaluating organisational interventions: cocreated program logic. This will help employers guide the evaluation of these changes and interventions. They provide two case studies illustrating how the process has been used in research, with lessons learned. Change is here to stay or as Churchill once suggested "to improve is to change, to be perfect is to change often". We only learn from exploring our change programmes and learn from our mistakes. Henry Ford once said, "Failure is only the opportunity to begin again more intelligently".

The new normal

The chapters in this book have provided us with various psychological insights on how to deal post COVID-19 in a range of people issues in the workplace, and during the subsequent recession. After months of lockdown as a result of COVID-19, and not being able to see our loved ones or going to work and having to work remotely, we are beginning to see the green shoots of a new normality! Yes, life will be different than it was pre-COVID, but in some regards we will have learned a great deal and can organise our lives to get better balance, to appreciate things and people we have taken for granted and to re-create the sense of community we have lost in leading our frenetic lives over the last couple of decades. We learned we can work remotely; we found out more about our work colleagues and forged closer relationships with them; we thought about our health and took daily exercise and we realised how important our work relationships were as we Skyped or Zoomed our colleagues, clients and suppliers.

Now that we are coming out of lockdown and re-entering the 'new normal', we can take control of our personal lives and work. What causes stress in life are uncertainty and lack of control. The virus will go away, but we need to remain vigilant and careful; we can however now gain control of our lives. There are a range of things we can do.

First, although we need to be careful over the next year about social distancing with work colleagues, we need to make sure that we are socially connected. Physical distancing but social connectedness! Human beings need social contact, so ensure you invest in people who matter but take precautions.

Second, if you are working, and you can, try to work more from home, going into a central office for occasional meetings and team building and to socialise with colleagues. Flexible working is firmly on everybody's agenda. This will help you forge closer relationships with your immediate family and particularly the community you live in. Evidence is as well that people who work more flexibly are more productive and job satisfied.

Third, we need to be kinder to our colleagues at work. Helping and supporting our work colleagues, clients and all those we work closely with, not only gives us a sense of purpose but also enhances our psychological health.

Fourth, we need to look after our physical health as well as our mental wellbeing. We have been in the habit over the COVID-19 lockdown of doing exercise at least once a day; this is good for you both from a physical health point of view but also from a psychological perspective as well. Let's continue this on in the post-COVID world.

Fifth, when the time is right, it is important that we stay socially connected with our work colleagues through social platforms when working from home, but also meeting them face to face when the virus is under control. It might be a while before we can relax social distancing, so continue to follow the advice and use your common sense in group gatherings – but life is about meeting our psychological and social needs, so face to face meetings will emerge.

Sixth, if you are feeling depressed or anxious, as many people are because of health fears and being isolated for so long, it is important to approach your boss and/or work colleagues and friends to talk about it. Sharing your fears and concerns with others can help you find a solution. Seeking social support will also alert work colleagues, friends and family that you are not coping, and they will then be able to help and support you.

Seventh, think about the planet and reduce your travel when you can. We do need holidays, and they will return, and we need holidays to be with family and friends in a less stressful context than work, it is about recovery and relaxation. Business travel for many, however, will decline as businesses need to save money, and we have social platforms like Zoom, Skype, etc. to meet our colleagues, clients, etc. without going too far afield – but not exclusively, as we need face to face contacts to meet our social needs.

These are just a few of the realities of life post COVID, and the psychological insights this volume provides. I hope you will find these contributions to be useful in providing a healthier and more productive workplace as we enter a 'new normal' world.

Professor Sir Cary L. Cooper, CBE
ALLIANCE Manchester Business School,
University of Manchester, UK

References

Cooper, C.L. & Lu, L. *Presenteeism at Work*. Cambridge: Cambridge University Press, 2018.
Hesketh, I. & Cooper. *Wellbeing at Work*. London: Kogan Page, 2019.
Office of National Statistics. *Social Impacts of Coronavirus (UK)*. London: ONS, May 2020.

1 The balanced communications diet for business

Principles for working smarter, not harder in a connected world

Nicola J. Millard

The problem of *workus interruptus*

Did you know that during an average working day we are allegedly interrupted once every three minutes (Mark et al., 2008) … oh, hang on my phone just beeped … now, where was I?

With agile and flexible working we may not be tethered to our offices or desks anymore, but the devices we have on us constantly have blurred the boundaries between our work life and the rest of our life. We have the pressure of responding to a multitude of beeps and buzzes whether we are in the boardroom, on the beach or in the bathroom. Communication is essential for healthy life and good business decisions, but being overwhelmed by communication is not. Just like food is essential for survival, too much of it can be bad for us.

Don't get me wrong, these technologies have made our working lives better in many ways. For a start, they put us in control of where, when and how we work. They are the foundation for flexible, agile and home working. They have changed the ways that we communicate and collaborate forever. The challenge isn't connection anymore; it is disconnection.

It may be easier to abstain from technology use outside the workplace but, when we often carry our offices around with us in our back pockets, disconnection can be challenging. It is more difficult than ever to define when we are working, and when we are not. This "always on" way of life can cause "techno-stress" – i.e. "stress caused by an inability to cope with the demands of organisational technology usage" (Tarafdar et al., 2010). To help combat this, we developed a set of simple principles – a "balanced communications diet for business" – to help us to become healthier and more productive in work.

When are we most productive?

"Productivity" is often defined in manufacturing terms as "the ratio of what is produced to what is required to produce it" (Hill, 1993). This is a simple concept when applied to a factory production line but, particularly when applied to knowledge work, it becomes more problematic. The only tangible input is the number of hours worked. Output is less easy to define. If people equate a clear email inbox, or constant availability on instant messenger, with productivity then that is probably what employees do all day. Is this really "productive work"?

In an attempt to understand productivity, BT and Cambridge University conducted a set of employee interviews (Mieczakowski et al., 2011). There were a wide variety of answers to the question *"Where, when and why are you most productive at work?"*

- *"I find I get a full day of work done between 6:00 and 9:30 in the morning. For my sanity as well, knowing I can get at least two productive hours of work in before breakfast, makes a huge difference to my day."*
- *"In the evening, hands down. Less interruptions and my natural time clock is at its peak then."*
- *"For ideas – it's before 9.30 am. For acting on those ideas, 10 am to 3 pm."*
- *"I need peace and quiet – interruptions just jumble my brain up and I get nothing done."*
- *"On a plane – it's the only safe haven now from calls and emails. Sadly, even that's changing now!"*
- *"I do all my thinking in the car – I have an hour's commute – once I get to the office it's all go, go, go! Do I want to work from home? No, I'd lose all that thinking time!"*
- *"I can tell you where I'm NOT productive – being tugged in all different places sitting in a 'team' set-up office with no privacy or physical barriers between myself and others."*

The general theme that emerges from these answers – aside from *"everyone is different"* – is that people regard themselves as most productive when they are free of interruption. This is often outside the office and the traditional 9-to-5 day. The problem is frequently that we can't get through the work for talking about the work. However, if you rephrase this question and ask people what motivates them about work over and above the money that they earn, they say that they *"like the people that they work with"*. These people, one assumes, are also generally the source of many of these interruptions!

A significant amount of research supports the idea that having time to think and reflect each day does a great deal for well-being, and constant interruptions can counter this (Mieczakowski et al., 2011; Tams et al., 2018; Galluch et al., 2015). This is the time that we seem to value, if the answers to these questions are to be believed. People who are always "plugged-in" often don't get this vital mental downtime. We all seem to recognise that we need peace and quiet sometimes to just think. But finding the time to do this can be easier said than done. We always seem to put a higher value on action rather than inaction. The value of reflection is underrated because business is so concerned with action and activity – things that are easy to measure – rather than thinking about action, which looks too much like staring into space.

This "cult of busyness" also means that we tend to get tugged in all directions during our working day. We can feel out of control. People are most likely to become enthusiastic about what they are doing when they are free to make decisions about the way that they do it. Classic psychology (Karasek & Theorell, 1990) tells us that high levels of demand and low levels of perceived control results in stress, burnout and emotional exhaustion.

Control is easier on some communication devices than others. It's easy to find the off switch on a laptop; but less so on a smart phone. Because we often can't be seen at our desks, or in the office anymore, there can be a pressure to be always on. Control can take other forms, though. Minimising distractions and interruptions could be one way of both taking control and becoming more productive.

Brain juggling

There is one thing that acts strongly against us simply choosing to switch off. Technology plays to the natural distractibility of human nature and our compulsion to embrace uncertainty and novelty (Fitz et al., 2019). Every time the new mail notification flashes up on screen, the red dot appears against an app, or our phone vibrates, we feel the need to take a look, regardless of what else we are doing. The vast majority of these alerts lead us to irrelevant, routine or junk stuff. However, there is the occasional "reward" – an important document or good news – that motivates us to keep checking for incoming messages even when we should really be paying attention to other things (like walking in a straight line or being at a meeting). In addition, the accomplishment we feel when we reach the end of our email inbox or send that witty tweet tends to be easier to achieve than doing all those other, more complex tasks on our "to do" list.

One problem with this is that the frequency of distraction is inversely correlated with productivity (Duke and Monta, 2017; Fitz et al., 2019). As we compulsively check incoming messages, the less productive we become. A number of studies have also cited a close relationship between stress and the amount of times we check our devices (e.g. Lee et al., 2014; Brod, 1984; Thomee et al., 2011). Turning alerts off is an obvious solution, but there is evidence that this can make people more anxious, as FOMO (Fear Of Missing Out) kicks in (Fitz et al., 2019). The most stressed individuals can even imagine "phantom" alerts and compulsively check their devices even when there is nothing coming in (Kruger & Djerf, 2017).

One of the big reasons that technology is more distracting now than it used to be is that the alerts from devices are increasingly social in nature. Devices alert us to messages, voicemails and even the locations of our friends and colleagues, whereas previously they might only send out alerts when they were out of batteries. These social alerts are hard to tune out. You can ignore the ping of a washing machine when it has finished a spin cycle, but you can't ignore your boss. This tends to result in us attempting to multitask.

Multitasking (attempting to perform two or more tasks simultaneously), or task switching (when you are interrupted mid-task) are effectively the mental equivalent of juggling. If you have ever closed your laptop down at the end of the day and found a multitude of half-finished email replies, chat sessions and half-completed documents, you have probably been doing one or the other. Academics have long known that task-switching has a detrimental effect on productivity, even for simple tasks (e.g. Rogers & Monsell, 1995). The results are even worse for complex tasks (e.g. Rubinstein et al., 2001). Although switch costs may be small, sometimes just a few tenths of a second per switch, they can add up to large amounts of time wasted when people switch repeatedly back and forth between tasks. Task switching can also impede memory and knowledge retention, particularly for interruptions mid-task. Interruptions reduce our ability to pay attention (Ophir et al., 2009), complete tasks, reduce task accuracy (Montag & Walla, 2016), and increases the time we take to complete tasks (Cellier & Eyrolle, 1992).

This means that multitasking may look productive, but it may actually take more time and involve more errors. Research from Stanford University (Ophir et al., 2009) has shown that people who regard themselves as good at multitasking are generally worse at judging the quality of information that they are reading and worse at recalling what they have done. This means that they are often less productive than people who are single taskers.

Multitasking can also be exhausting (Mark et al., 2008; Monicque et al., 2009). Paying attention to one thing whilst doing another means that we need to do more work to maintain any level of attention on either task. Sitting in a meeting doing email on your phone generally means either the meeting or the email gets short shrift. The lesson here? The average person is generally unaware of the cognitive effect that technology is having on their life.

Ultimately, much of this boils down to stress because of the sheer number of things that are simultaneously competing for our attention – "information overload" (Tarafdar et al., 2010). Being able to prioritise in overload situations is extremely difficult and can result in us going up a number of productivity cul-de-sacs. Having the self-control to close everything down and concentrate on a single task until it is finished is probably the biggest challenge but the key to better productivity.

How do we prefer to communicate at work?

Ultimately, old fashioned face-to-face communication still emerges as essential for building trust, and delivering important or emotionally sensitive messages (Pentland, 2015). But getting people in the same room together can be almost impossible, especially in highly virtualised and globalised businesses. Inevitably, much of business today is conducted over digital communication channels.

Text-based communications – especially chat – tends to be a favourite for pure information exchange (Hickman & Davies, 2018). It is an easy way to get messages to a lot of people with minimal effort. But it's difficult to convey much in terms of nuance and emotion in text, unless you pepper it with emoticons.

Text-based communications can also create excessive demands on the receivers of them. This is sometimes called "techno-overload" (Tarafdar et al., 2010). As technology makes us more productive and more efficient, things that used to take days now take minutes. This can create a sudden influx of demand on us, can lead managers to communicate more than is necessary (Davis, 2002) and get more information than they can process and use effectively (Fisher & Wesolkowski, 1999). We also tend to become increasingly unable to identify information that is actually useful, rather than spam.

This often results in us getting both tired and stressed, as well as working longer hours. The productivity benefits of agile and flexible working can potentially be displaced by the resulting pressure to keep on top of things. This "techno-invasion" (Tarafdar et al., 2010) can result in people feeling as if they are tethered permanently to work. They may leave the office, but they can't leave the office behind.

Being "always on" can significantly impinge on family time. The "speed trap" of quick reflex responses has brought pressure to respond immediately. This belief tends to create a false sense of urgency, puts pressure on us to respond fast (with no time to think carefully about our responses) and means that we can spend more time reading and responding to it than actually getting any other work done.

This sense of urgency can have a negative impact on the quality of decision-making (Perlow et al., 2002). Speed and quality are two key variables when people make important decisions, and they often come into conflict. Fast decisions are not always ideal, but more decisions are, of necessity, being made quickly. Faster communication provides more information for decision-makers to use, but their decisions might lack detail or adequate consideration. Combine that with the inevitable shortening of attention spans and we get a shallow, 180-character elevator pitch style of communication. Worse still, key people may not respond in time and decisions are then made without their potentially critical input.

The cost to users is also a factor which needs to be considered. In order to communicate with others in the past there was a cost incurred by both the sender and receiver of information. This was in terms of effort and often financially as well. Today, people can send huge amounts of material to others quickly and with almost zero additional cost. It is easier than ever before to burden other people with a deluge of information that might be important but that they never see because of inbox overload.

The great thing – and the problem – with email is that it covers a kind of middle ground between other more instant forms of communication (chat, social media, telephone, meetings) and more traditional written communications like post (Newport, 2019). For one thing, you can communicate with a lot of people at a single click of the "send" key without the need for them to be there, or the niceties and small talk that frequently occur with more synchronous forms of communication, like the phone. The fact that it leaves an audit trail is also flagged as an advantage (Mieczakowski et al., 2011).

The demise of email has been long forecast, but old channels often stick around. It is gradually being eclipsed by chat, though. Chat is very much where it's at in the consumer space – with the proliferation of messaging apps such as WhatsApp, WeChat and Facebook Messenger. Inevitably, many of these tools are being brought into the workplace (Hickman & Davies, 2018). Chat can have some advantages. It is short, easy and quick but, as a tool of mass distraction, it still has many of the same disadvantages as email.

Social media has also been mooted as the ultimate collaboration tool within enterprises. Its significant strength is that you don't actually have to know who to contact in order to message them and it can cross organisational silos (and defy spam filters). Finding the right person to talk to without cc'ing the whole company is sometimes very difficult in the email universe.

However, social media also has similar weaknesses in terms of information overload and as a task interrupter, with some people reporting "stream stress" as they attempt to keep up on Twitter, Facebook, Yammer, LinkedIn, Instagram and the multitude of other social tools. The danger is that we may just end up with a raft of emails being replaced with a stream of messages from multiple different sources.

Introducing the balanced communications diet for business

The way that we work has been changed fundamentally by the technologies that we use. Ways of communication with others have changed. Knowledge access has increased, but being awash with too much data has threatened our ability both to process everything and also to acquire new knowledge. There are clear positives and negatives here.

This is where well-being at work comes in. Well-being is defined by the Cambridge Dictionary as "the state of feeling healthy and happy". It is more than just personal happiness and takes into account factors such as sense of purpose and direction. Those who report "techno-stress" at work frequently feel overwhelmed or constantly distracted by communications technology and are more likely to report lower perceptions of well-being (Tarafdar et al., 2010).

Throwing away technology is neither desirable, nor practical, but changing our use of it could result in better productivity and more time to ourselves. To improve well-being, we need to look at how we are using technology and whether or not we can improve our perception of control over its use.

The main problem highlighted by the BT/Cambridge research was that ubiquitous connectivity made it easy to check on things at work at any time of the day (Mieczakowski et al., 2011). Moreover, a "quick phone check" could easily turn into several hours of use.

What can we do to achieve a better communications diet for business? There are five things to consider:

- Location
- Rules
- Awareness
- Education
- Balance.

Location

Location is becoming a very key aspect to ensuring that business communication is effective. Just because we *can* work anywhere doesn't mean we *should*.

Work can literally be defined by space. With the rise of flexible working, that space may not be within the four walls of an office anymore. If you live and work in the same place, establishing boundaries between the "office" and the "home" can be important. Some flexible workers can go to extreme strategies to separate the two. Anecdotally, I know people who have established their office in a shed in their back garden, dress in a suit during working hours, or work from co-working spaces or coffee shops. Closing the office door at the end of the day and leaving the phone and laptop behind is a powerful way of exerting control. The same rule applies when you are on holiday.

Location can also be determined by the device. Doing a considered reply to a complex topic is probably better done on a better and bigger screen than on a smartphone – so may not be appropriate whilst you are on the move. It is often easier to send a one-sentence message on a smart phone because you are attempting to type using a tiny keypad whilst squinting at a small screen. Many of these curt replies can cause significant misunderstandings and result in yet more messages to distract you.

Another way of exerting a degree of control over location is to move from a default of always on, to choosing when you are on. Turn your phone off when in meetings so that there is no temptation to be distracted by your device silently flashing at you at inappropriate moments. Turn alerts off rather than having them continuously beckoning you to look at them. That way you have to consciously log on to access it rather than simply flick from one app to another. Disconnect when you are doing tasks that require concentration so that you are forced to concentrate on a single task rather than succumb to the temptation to surf.

Research from the universities of Würzburg, Germany, and Nottingham Trent, UK, has gone so far as to suggest that removing the smartphone from the room you are in entirely could significantly improve productivity (Carolus et al., 2018).

Rules

Establish rules for yourself. Set times when you are "on" and when you are "off". Some people are choosing to go back to an old-fashioned feature phone with no internet connectivity, so that they can't access online content. Others have taken to carrying two devices around; one for work and one for personal activities. Aside from the inconvenience of an extra slab of technology to lug about, this can strictly partition the working day from family time.

Ironically one thing that is coming along to help us manage our technology is more technology. Having a virtual desktop in the cloud for work can ensure that you are logged in to that space by choice rather than by default. There are also intelligent personal assistants which can automatically tag and prioritise incoming messages as urgent, non-urgent, spam, or personal.

Using presence information to define times when you are available for interruption can provide people with a guide as to when and how is the best time to contact you. Appearing offline on instant messenger is not a crime and "busy" really does mean that you don't want to be interrupted. Similarly, setting time limits for doing email can also prove beneficial. Some people schedule email free days once a week.

Some corporates and countries have gone one step further and imposed rules to help employees to turn off. European countries such as France have established a "right to turn off" policy as part of their flexible working initiatives. Some companies will only allow employees access to their email accounts half an hour before and half an hour after a shift. Others automatically delete email when people are on leave. These top-down strategies may not work for all organisations, however, particularly those who operate flexible working hours, or work across global boundaries and time zones.

Awareness

Understand how you are using technology when you are working. Awareness of use is the key to achieving balance and well-being when using communications technology, largely because most people appear to be unaware just how much they use it and how habitual their use is. Try recording the ways in which you are using technology at work for a few days. Some apps will automatically record screen time for you to save you having to think about it. You can then try to aim for a more ideal level, whatever you define that level to be.

Education

This is really around establishing guidelines and cultural norms around acceptable use of communication channels. Establishing conventions such as "no email after 5.30 pm", asking "is this the right channel for this message" and allowing individuals to broadcast their communication preferences are all part of the process of educating the workforce.

Many organisations are establishing organisational communication etiquette and even providing training courses on the appropriate use of communication and clear language within their business. Even simple things like establishing rules on when, or when not, to use "reply to all" in email messages or how to construct meaningful subject lines can make a huge difference. Behaviours often come from the top, so it is critical for leaders to display appropriate communication behaviours themselves (Schwartz & Porath, 2014). They shouldn't bombard their people with email at all times of the day and night, micro-manage their employees on instant messenger, or schedule meetings at anti-social hours (particularly challenging when global virtual teams are involved as it's always five o'clock somewhere).

Balance

As with everything else, moderation is key. Moderation of communications technology, whether it is by location, rules or something else, is ultimately a way to achieve a certain sense of balance. Self-control plays a critical part in this. If we want to become more productive and lessen the potential negative impact of technology, we need to make a conscious effort to control how we use it. The larger problem is that we really are not aware of when we are in control of technology and when technology is in control of us.

There is no perfect way to exert self-control. We are better at controlling ourselves in certain situations than others. People who are more easily distracted by technology must, first, become aware of it before they can start to control their behaviour.

However, behavioural economists will tell you that self-control may be less straightforward than we may think (Ariely & Wertenbroch, 2002). What looks like exquisite self-control can actually just be an instance of rule-following. For example, if someone is told that they must check their email only twice a day and then does so, they are not exhibiting traditional self-control, but are simply following a rule. Self-control has to do with being aware of the potential long-term consequences of an action and acting accordingly, even when the short-term consequences would be pleasurable. Rule-following only requires us to do what we are told. While self-control will likely play a big role in how much modern technology affects any one individual, it is important to keep in mind how self-control is characterised and how it differs between individuals.

Many of the concerns about what communications technology is doing to us are about the degree to which it stops us talking to each other in a traditional way. Emailing or messaging the person sitting opposite us makes no sense and yet we often do exactly that. This could be due to lack of privacy in the office space we are in (Bernstein & Turban, 2018), or simply that we can establish an audit trail of the conversation.

Establishing a balance around communications use at work is vital. Anyone who has sat through a conference doing their emails only to suddenly realise they have no concept of what has actually happened in the real world needs to ask themselves why they were at that event. This is sometimes called "continuous partial attention" (Hemp, 2009). Establishing boundaries for acceptable use of communications technologies is important. In meetings, both face-to-face and virtual, switching everything off should be acceptable behaviour.

However, the point that balance is achieved is probably unique to each and every one of us. Some people feel lost without their smartphones, while others relish time out. Regardless of your preference, there is evidence that having at least some technology down time is beneficial to well-being (Tarafdar et al., 2010; Thomée et al., 2011; Fitz et al., 2019). Taking a tech break can also reduce feelings of dependence on technology (Carolus et al., 2018).

Recommendations

As employees further blur the lines between work and play by working flexible hours, home working, or bringing their own devices, apps and tools to work, there is a risk that switching off from the digital business world entirely will become more and more difficult. The productivity penalties of being "always on" are still being uncovered. Indeed, one recommendation for future research is to reinvent and redefine productivity in the context of the digital workplace. Measuring the number of hours worked, or sick days logged is easy to do, but not necessarily relevant for a rigorous investigation of productivity in an era where people work more flexibly and virtually. Establishing measures, or proxies, for productivity and connecting them to areas such as well-being are vital, but extremely difficult (especially for knowledge workers).

The impact of multitasking is another area of concern which deserves more research attention since it can be a significant time devourer in an increasingly distracting world. Mistaking activity for productivity – whatever that means in a digital world – may mean that we have little time to "unplug" and unwind.

Leadership inevitably plays a huge part in this. Leaders need to role model a balanced workstyle in order for their employees to do the same.

All of this becomes more important as we consider the future world of work. Artificial Intelligence (AI) may help us become more productive but it may also cause more intensification of our work (Waytz, 2019). It is likely to leave human workers with an increasingly messy, complex, emotive and even less quantifiable workload. This means that there is likely to be more focus in the future on employee well-being, burn out prevention and the importance of down time.

Ultimately, it is up to us to establish a balance that suits us as individuals. This means that consideration of principles such as the "balanced communications diet" – i.e. location, rules, awareness, education and balance – will become increasingly important to help individuals to work smarter, not harder.

Acknowledgements

The author would like to thank Mary Lumkin, Jeff Patmore, Anna Mieczakowski, Tanya Goldhaber and John Clarkson for their work on the original "Balanced Communications Diet" research, which inspired "The Balanced Communications Diet for Business" paper.

References

Ariely, D. & Wertenbroch, K. (2002), Procrastination, deadlines and performance: Self-control by precommitment, psychological science, *American Psychological Society*, *13*(3), May, 219–244.

Bernstein, E.S. & Turban, S. (2018), The impact of the "open" workspace on human collaboration, *Philosophical Transactions of the Royal Society B Biological Sciences*, *373*, http://doi.org/10.1098/rstb.2017.0239

Brod, C. (1984), *Technostress: The human cost of the computer revolution*, Reading, MA: Addison-Wesley.

Carolus, A., Binder, J.F., Muench, R., Schmidt, C., Schneider, F. & Buglass, S. (2018), Smartphones as digital companions: Characterizing the relationship between users and their phones, *New Media and Society*, *21*(4), 914–938.

Cellier, J. & Eyrolle, H. (1992), Interference between switched tasks. *Ergonomics*, *35*(1), 25–36.

Davis, G. (2002), Anytime/anyplace computing and the future of knowledge work, *Communications of the ACM*, *45*(2), 67–73.

Duke, É. & Monta, C. (2017), Smartphone addiction, daily interruptions and self-reported productivity, *Addictive Behaviours Reports*, *6*(December), 90–95.

Fisher, W. & Wesolkowski, S. (1999), Tempering technostress, *IEEE Technology and Society Magazine*, *18*(1), 28–33.

Fitz, N., Kushlev, K., Jagannathan, R., Lewis, T., Paliwal, D. & Ariely, D. (2019), Batching smartphone notifications can improve well-being, *Computers in Human Behaviour*, *101*(December), 84–94.

Galluch, P.S., Grover, V. & Thatcher, J.B. (2015), Interrupting the workplace: Examining stressors in an information technology context, *Journal of the Association for Information Systems*, *16*(1), 1–47.

Hemp, P. (2009), Death by information overload, *Harvard Business Review*, *87*(September), 49–53.

Hickman, M. & Davies, J. (2018), *People, productivity and the digital workplace: How mobile and collaboration services can boost productivity*, Digital Employee Research 2018, BT White Paper, https://www.globalservices.bt.com/en/insights/whitepapers/people-productivity-in-digital-workplace

Hill, T. (1993), *Manufacturing Strategy: The Strategic Management of the Manufacturing Function* (2nd ed.), London: Open University/Macmillan.

Karasek, R.A. & Theorell, T.G. (1990), *Healthy Work: Stress, Productivity and the Reconstruction of Working Life*, New York: Basic Books.

Kruger, J.M. & Djerf, J.M. (2017), Bad vibrations? Cell phone dependency predicts phantom communication experiences, *Computers in Human Behaviour*, *70*(May), 360–364.

Lee, Y., Chang, C., Lin, Y. & Cheng, Z. (2014), The dark side of smartphone usage: Psychological traits, compulsive behaviors and techno-stress, *Computers in Human Behaviour*, *31*(February), 373–383.

Mark, G., Gudith, D. & Klocke, U. (2008), The cost of interrupted work: More speed and stress, *Proceedings of CHI 08, Proceedings of the SIGCHI Conference on Human Factors in Computing Systems*, New York: ACM, pp. 107–110.

Mieczakowski, A., Goldhaber, T. & Clarkson, J. (2011), *Culture, Communication and Change: Report on an Investigation of the Use and Impact of Modern Media and Technology in Our Lives*, Cambridge, UK: Engineering Design Centre, University of Cambridge/BT, https://www-edc.eng.cam.ac.uk/downloads/culturebook.pdf

Monicque, M., Lorista, B., Bezdana, E., ten Caat, M., Spana, M.M., Roerdink, J.B.T.M. & Maurits, N.M. (2009), The influence of mental fatigue and motivation on neural network dynamics; an EEG coherence study, *Brain Research*, *1270*(May), 95–106.

Montag, C. & Walla, P. (2016), Carpe diem instead of losing your social mind: Beyond digital addiction and why we all suffer from digital overuse, *Cogent Psychology*, *3*(1).

Newport, C. (2019), Was e-mail a mistake? The mathematics of distributed systems suggests that meetings might be better, *The New Yorker*, August 6.

Ophir, E., Nass, C. & Wagner, A.D. (2009), Cognitive control in media multitaskers, *PNAS*, *106*(37), 15 September, 15583–15587, www.pnas.org_cgi_doi_10.1073_pnas.0903620106

Pentland, A. (2015), *Social Physics: How Social Networks Can Make Us Smarter*, New York: Penguin Random House.

Perlow, L., Okhuyson, G. & Repenning, N. (2002), The speed trap: Exploring the relationship between decision making and the temporal context, *Academy of Management Journal*, *45*(5), October, 931–955.

Rogers, R.D. & Monsell, S. (1995), Costs of a predictable switch between simple cognitive tasks, *Journal of Experimental Psychology*, *124*(2), 207.

Rubinstein, J., Evans, J. & Meyer, D. (2001), Executive control of cognitive processes in task switching, *Journal of Experimental Psychology Human Perception & Performance*, *27*(4), September, 763–797.

Schwartz, T. & Porath, C. (2014), Your boss's work-life balance matters as much as your own, *Harvard Business Review*, July 10.

Tams, S., Grover, V. & Thatcher, J.B. (2018), Concentration, competence, confidence, and capture: An experimental study of age, interruption-based technostress, and task performance, *Journal of the Association for Information Systems*, *19*(9), 857–890.

Tarafdar, M., Tu, Q. & Ragu-Nathan, T.S. (2010), Impact of technostress on end-user satisfaction and performance, *Journal of Management Information Systems*, *27*(3), Winter, 303–334.

Thomée, S., Härenstam, A. & Hagberg, M. (2011), Mobile phone use and stress, sleep disturbances, and symptoms of depression among young adults – a prospective cohort study, *BMC Public Health*, *11*, article 66, https://bmcpublichealth.biomedcentral.com/articles/10.1186/1471-2458-11-66

Waytz, A. (2019), Leisure is our killer app, *MIT Sloan Management Review*, Summer, https://sloanreview.mit.edu/article/leisure-is-our-killer-app

2

WELLBEING

The fundamentals

Ian Hesketh and Sir Cary L. Cooper

Introduction

Having made a case for wellbeing in the previous chapter, we now move on to suggest a framework for getting started with wellbeing in the workplace, with these three fundamental tenets: personal resilience, creating the right environment and aligning your leaders. In this chapter we will reference quite a bit of academic research, which we hope will provide a further source of reading and an evidence base for our claims. Although some of these studies, like most academic literature, may feature contested views, we consider them to be the best sources of reference at the time of writing and therefore include them for information. All three of our tenets are discussed in depth, with supporting evidence from the field, to provide a framework from which teams, departments, business units and organisations can build an effective wellbeing approach in the workplace. Evidence is exhibited of an approach that is grounded on a successful model that has been proven to work in practice in the UK public service sector. Examples are given of how creating the right environment can impact significantly on the health and wellbeing of the workforce. How the physiological, psychological, sociological and financial aspects of wellbeing all have a part to play will be modelled in this chapter. These things are done through the actions of good/ethical leaders/managers, together with the personal resilience of employees and correct amounts of work–life balance, healthy lifestyles and meaning and purpose in working life.

What we suggest is that you try all this out in whatever work setting you happen to be. Nothing is more convincing than to see theoretical models working in practice, and here is where we posit this book will be of real use to those either studying or practising. Particular relevancy is to be seen in the utilisation of the model above. The first step is to explore the content of this to see if it resonates with the workforce you are interested in. We find this initial enquiry stage is

FIGURE 3.1   Organisational recipe for wellbeing

Source: Copyright © Hesketh, 2014.

particularly important. It also provides confidence that the content accords with people. Towards the end of this book we hear accounts from leaders in organisations who have actually put it into practice, and hear how effective strategies on wellbeing are in real-life public sector working environments. These accounts give readers an opportunity to test their thoughts against those of others, to see if the themes resonate, and if the working environment can be improved by subtle incremental changes in practice, perhaps coupled with having a growth mindset.

Personal resilience

Personal resilience is broadly viewed as the antidote to stress. The discovery of stress is commonly attributed to Hans Selye, who in 1935 identified the syndrome in laboratory rats (Viner, 1999; Cooper, 2004). He later suggested the notion that there may be good stress, which he termed *eustress*, as opposed to *distress* (Selye, 1984). Since then the theory has been developed, and a contemporary view of stress is often seen as being the point after which the amount of pressure a person is under exceeds their ability to cope, while conceding that some pressure is actually good for you. There may be a different 'set point' for everyone, dependent on skills, capability, personality, etc. 'It has to be recognized that stress is dynamic and, in a rapidly changing environment, is unlikely to ever disappear completely, but needs to be regularly monitored and addressed.' (Cooper and Cartwright, 1997, p.12). As well as traditional descriptions associated with stress through too much work, i.e. overload, employees can experience stress by having too little to do, causing boredom, apathy and frustration, which can be equally stressful (Palmer and Cooper, 2010). Figure 3.2 shows this relationship and is adapted from the seminal work of Yerkes and Dodson.

These dimensions form the basis of resilience programmes that have been developed to equip workers with the necessary tools to recognise and act in respect of their own personal circumstances. It would seem, then, that if stress is ever present, so too should be mechanisms to confront it. Resilience is the prime mechanism,

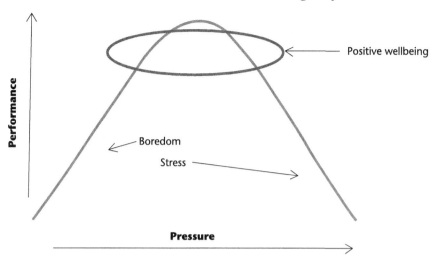

FIGURE 3.2 Performance–pressure relationship

Source: Adapted from Yerkes and Dodson (1908).

and therefore those equipped with the knowledge and skill to be aware of, and improve, their resilience ought to function better in the workplace. Resilience is a combination of personal characteristics and learned skills. These learned skills could include thinking differently, for example using CBT techniques to reframe negative thoughts. They can include having the ability to deal with both success and failure, and developing a positive attribution style. Other learned skills can centre on coping strategies, self-mastery, making the most of personal (signature) strengths and learning to work smarter. All these are proven to increase personal resilience.

In terms of personal resilience, speaking in a UK radio interview, the President of the Royal College of Psychiatrists in the UK, Sir Simon Wessely, noted that actually people are a bit tougher than we generally think (BBC, 2017). Basing his argument on research with Second World War survivors, he proposed that, in relation to research on modern day terrorist attacks, most people do not require any mental help assistance in overcoming traumatic events, and in fact some of the interventions can make the subjects worse off. He argued that interventions such as post-event diffusing sessions were subject to randomised control trials, a robust research methodology used in the majority of scientific research, and seemed to actually have a detrimental effect.

The word 'resilience' itself has roots in the Latin verb *resilire* – to rebound, to return to normal. The various definitions share talk about elasticity, so notions of being stretched and returning to shape could be conjured up. In Figure 3.1 (see p. 34) we have split resilience into two features: coping with adversity and being able to bounce back. We will unpick those a little later, but first we will take a look at the views some academics have given about what resilience is. We have provided some of the more popular interpretations of resilience in a workplace context but concede there are a good deal more out there. However, to cohere with the narrative appended to the model, we draw upon some of the following explanations.

In terms of the public sector, a great deal of research on resilience has focused on the emergency and caring professions such as the police (Paton, 2006), army (Cornum, 2012), ambulance service (Gayton and Lovell, 2012), nursing (Zander et al., 2013), and social work (Grant and Kinman, 2013). We assume that this is probably because of the high levels of stress experienced in these roles, all of which draw heavily on emotional labour. We will link this to *empathy* later in the chapter. For now we will try to highlight some of the global interpretations of resilience that accord with our own model above, and which can be both measured and analysed by survey instruments. This allows us to effectively establish what works in terms of addressing personal resilience, which is discussed in Chapter 4.

In a US study aimed at identifying and treating individuals at risk of post-trauma, Haglund et al. suggest resilience refers to the 'ability to successfully adapt to stressors, maintaining psychological wellbeing in the face of adversity' (2007, p.899). Two of the co-authors of this paper were Southwick and Charney, who developed a 'resilience prescription' founded upon experiences of prisoners of war (Southwick and Charney, 2012b). They were particularly interested in how some people were able to bounce back from adversity and some were unable to do so, which even extended to people who had experienced the same traumatic events.

Ann Masten from the University of Minnesota, writing about global perspectives on resilience in children following natural disasters, suggests it is 'the capacity of a dynamic system to adapt successfully to disturbances that threaten system function, viability, or development' (2014, p.6). Her study drew on reports from the United Nations about post-disaster coping after events such as tsunamis, earthquakes, conflicts and other disasters. She was interested in what makes individuals resilient and who stays well and recovers well, and how, using what is arguably the most extreme of samples to study. She concluded, positively, that resilience is made up of ordinary processes, and a book followed that detailed her work, aptly called *Ordinary Magic: Resilience in Development* (2014).

Larry Mallack, researching resilience amongst healthcare providers in the US and developing a Workplace Resilience Instrument, described resilience as 'the ability of an individual or organization to expeditiously design and implement positive adaptive behaviors matched to the immediate situation, while enduring minimal stress' (1998, p.148).

Fred Luthans, who writes largely about positive organisational behaviour and developing and managing psychological strengths, defines resilience as the 'positive psychological capacity to rebound or bounce back from adversity, uncertainty, conflict, failure or even positive change, progress and increased responsibility' (2002, p.702). Luthans is of a view that optimistic, energetic people who enjoy life can be a major attribute to an organisation, a view we would echo. Luthans' definition highlights the well-known and important 'bouncing back' (or rebounding) aspect of resilience and is useful in drawing attention to the extensive need for resilience in both positive (opportunities or advancement) and negative (dealing with adversity) experiences in the workplace. He makes mention of bouncing back in terms of something that can be learned or enhanced through mastery. Luthans' notion about the ability to 'bounce back' from adversity, or rebound, seems to make perfect sense, although the origins of the phrase 'bouncebackability' appear to be ascribed to the 'great philosopher' Ian Dowie (a UK football pundit) in his descriptions of a woeful season for Crystal Palace (a UK football team)!

Brigadier General Rhonda Cornum (Cornum, 2012) suggests that the things that enable a person to 'bounce back' are not all due to an individual's make-up, and effective coping strategies can be learned and developed. Up until recently Dr Rhonda Cornum, a surgeon, was Director of the US Joint Soldier Fitness Programme. This programme introduced pre-deployment resilience training, amongst other things, for members of the armed forces and subsequently their families. Both Cornum and Casey (of VUCA fame) were heavily involved with the development and implementation of this ground-breaking programme. The careers of both these soldiers make for fascinating reading, Cornum was shot down in a Black Hawk helicopter during the Gulf War and held prisoner, giving her first-hand experience of the ultimate in resilience challenges.

As emotions are critical, research on emotional resilience has linked people's physical and emotional reactions and seeks to explain why the body reacts in the way it does and to offer useful strategies to help overcome the negative reactions and effects. Douglas Paton, who studied trauma in police officers' claims in relation to critical incident stress, such as the well-known condition of PTSD, stated that there can be 'both positive (e.g., posttraumatic growth) and negative outcomes (e.g., learned avoidance of threat situations)' (2006, p.198).

Dr Sam Goldstein, an American neuropsychologist, shifted the approach in his work with children from that of trying to find out what was wrong to studying what methods people could employ to overcome some of the adversity we have discussed. His focus was on how children who have experienced huge levels of adversity then went on to lead successful and happy lives by fostering strength, hope and optimism. His observations were that increasing stress, pressure and demands on schoolchildren (in the US) were leading to health disorders, and a huge rise in depression amongst school-age children. He concluded, in support of what we have already established to a large extent, that resilience held the keys to solving many of these problems. Goldstein also suggested that resilience, which he described as the ability to cope and feel competent, could overcome a genetic predisposition. His argument was that lived experiences, understanding of ourselves and the ability to think positively and overcome day-to-day challenges in life could supersede biological make-up.

One of the areas receiving a burgeoning amount of attention in public services, and to some extent the private sector, is investment in employee resilience training. With entrepreneurs across the globe positing the benefits to organisations, it seems to be a growth industry. But, as we will suggest here, if organisations are going to invest money, time and effort into resilience training, it is better to take the time to establish the needs of both the organisation and the individuals working within it before embarking on the journey. Having published numerous academic papers on the subject, we can say with some authority that such an important decision, in terms of both financial and emotional investment, ought to be made carefully and considerately. If the training, delivered professionally and in the context of the working environment, is to be effective, we suggest it is well worth investing in a professional outfit that has credibility and a reputation for quality. Some of our own research has shown negligible impact when this is not so. However, incredible results, including sustainable performance over time, are achievable when the training is delivered professionally.

One area that has been contested over recent years is whether it is worthwhile for organisations to train up their own people to deliver resilience training, and the pros and cons associated with this practice. In many public services, centralised L&D and HRM departments may find themselves being asked to deliver this sort of service. We suggest that, unless there are professionals in those departments, it is better left to the experts. However, it seems the benefits of refresher training and such may be appropriately delivered in discursive in-house sessions, perhaps in the vein of peer support.

Creating the right environment – engagement

Creating the right environment in the workplace is no easy task, perhaps one of the toughest managers face. It takes a lot of effort and a deep understanding of the concepts at play. The *culture*, the *identity*, the *organisational paradigm* – these are all phrases that can be associated with creating the right environment. The links between *resilience*, *leadership* and the relationship with *discretionary effort*, and the importance of effective *engagement*, are all academically robust and play a key role in getting things right. We use the construct of *engagement* as a central theme to pull these elements together and illustrate how those charged can create, and influence others in creating, a working environment congruent with employee wellbeing. Engagement has become one of the highest priorities for organisations around the globe, but whilst managers are fully aware of the importance of a highly engaged workforce, very few seem to understand what practices drive and sustain high levels of engagement.

In terms of *engagement*, it may be prudent to explain what exactly we are talking about here, what definition we are attributing to it in a working context. People have a choice about how much of themselves they offer up at work, what sort of level of investment they have in the organisation, and the function it performs. Closely associated with discretionary effort, employees must feel that their work has meaning and purpose, that it is worthwhile, and that somehow they contribute to the collective effort. In a study of engagement and burnout in Spanish workers and students at a university, Schaufeli et al. (from Utrecht University in the Netherlands) offered a definition of workplace engagement as 'a positive, fulfilling, work-related state of mind that is characterized by vigor, dedication, and absorption' (2002, p.74). What is particularly interesting, although in a fairly negative light, is that their study noted that the majority of academic study focused on the negative outcomes; they suggested a ratio of 15:1. So they looked at what the positive outcomes were, and how they were brought about, largely through the lens of engagement. So *engagement* can be a way we view interactions positively. Each of their elements of vigor, dedication and absorption have further descriptions that are closely related to Positive Psychology, such as *flow*, described by Martin Seligman (Seligman, 2003), and *subjective wellbeing or happiness* (Diener, 2000). We will discuss the seminal work of Seligman and Diener later in the book.

Robertson and Cooper (2010) proposed that, to maintain high levels of sustainable employee engagement, employee wellbeing should also be high, and this can be achieved through 'full engagement' and not just a commitment-based (organisational) view of the concept. In support, an analysis of sickness in hospital employees in Copenhagen, Denmark, found that those who experienced high levels of meaningfulness in their job and those who had trusting relationships with their immediate supervisors were far less likely to take sickness absence (Suadicani et al., 2014). Interestingly this study also looked at when an employee has an *intention to leave* an organisation and the relationship this has with their sickness absence. We have suggested that *intention to leave* does not automatically result in actually leaving but can result in employees effectively 'playing up' if they are in this state of mind, i.e. disengaged from work and/or the workplace. As alluded to earlier, in terms of sickness absence, research indicates that engaged workers take on average 2.69 and the disengaged take 6.19 days sickness per year (Rayton et al., 2012). We would suggest that this doubling between engaged and disengaged is a great means by which to view the benefits that effective engagement can provide to an organisation. These figures originate from the well-known Engage for Success programme in the UK, which reported that only a third of workers in the UK are engaged. They also suggest that engagement directly impacts on productivity and performance.

There is an acknowledgement that employees can, in fact, be too committed and too engaged with their work. One should also take care not to relate working hard with *burnout*. We suggest burnout, or mental weariness as it has been referred to, occurs when working at 85–100% of one's capacity over long periods of time, i.e. as almost the norm. It has been established that burnout is not the antipode of engagement (Schaufeli and Bakker, 2004). Bakker, in research carried out in four different service organisations in the Netherlands, describes people who are too engaged and too committed as 'workaholics' or 'work addicts' and distinguishes them from employees who experience authentic engagement in their work, who, they argue, have outside interests (societal wellbeing) and find their work enjoyable and fun (Bakker and Demerouti, 2008); this is similar to the concept of being in 'flow', according to Seligman, who describes it as 'being at one with the music, time stopping, and the loss of self-consciousness during an absorbing activity' (2011, p.11). These 'addicts' may materialise through concepts such as *presenteeism*, when an employee attends work whilst they are actually unwell or puts in 'face time' to indicate their dedication to work (Johns, 2010); or *leaveism*, a term we introduced, following research, to describe when an employee takes part of their annual leave entitlement to have time off work when they are actually unwell, or who take work on holiday or home that they cannot complete in their contracted hours (Hesketh and Cooper, 2014). Therefore it is important to delineate, and establish, what behaviour it is that employees are exhibiting: *highly engaged* or *addicted*? These concepts are not easily defined or interpreted and, as with leaveism, we note that our conceptualisation can be viewed through either a positive or a negative lens. For example, it could be argued that employees should not feel the need to take annual leave if they feel unwell. However, for a variety of reasons, employees feel better taking this route. Now, we do not condone some of the reasons offered; for example, the fear of being dismissed or viewed in a bad light is clearly not a good thing. But, if employees feel an overwhelming need to show loyalty and are proud of an unblemished sickness record (albeit not authentic), then this option may actually make them feel better. Who are we to judge? And likewise with taking work home – although clearly a sign of workload overload, some employees may wish to take their time and not feel hurried. It may be their way of reducing internal stress levels, so they may show high self-awareness traits? Again, the reasons are unclear, and probably very subjective dependent on circumstances, so we may reserve judgement until further research has been carried out to establish why this occurs in the workplace. One thing is for sure, and that is that it is prevalent, and it would appear that the higher up in an organisation an employee gets, the more likely it is that it will occur.

A US study concluded that high performance, positive attitudes and lower staff turnover are all cited as positive outcomes of a highly engaged workforce (Crawford et al., 2010), whilst research in the UK police suggested that employees who are masking illness or taking work on holiday may actually be working over their limits of resilience (Hesketh et al., 2015b). In research carried out in Austria, Gerich suggests that high workload seems to predict sickness presence, whereas fear of job loss appears to promote leaveism (2015). Wiley (2009) suggests that as few as a third of workers are engaged in the UK. He claims that the leadership behaviours and practices can be very different in organisations seeking a high engagement workforce, evoking trust and confidence in senior leaders, which he argues leads to high performance as a direct consequence. He concedes this high performance is delivered, to a large extent, via discretionary effort. It appears that once again leadership plays a key role, especially the line management of individuals (their immediate supervision); they are critical to creating the right environment for employees to engage proactively (Hesketh et al., 2014b). These environmental aspects were discussed in great detail in the (UK) government sponsored review of workplace engagement mentioned earlier (MacLeod and Clarke, 2009). Line managers are not only required to know their staff in almost familial ways, but it is incumbent on leaders to ensure work is also challenging. Crawford et al. argue that work demands that are viewed as a *hindrance* by employees are related negatively to engagement, but work demand that is *challenging* (even if difficult) is positively related to engagement (2010, p.835). We could also make similar links to conceptualisations of presenteeism and leaveism, whereby the underlying rationale directs the perceived orientation of the subject. So in many ways both phenomena can be viewed positively or negatively, dependent on the thought processes of the employees themselves. This is similar to the views of discretion and discretionary effort.

We now take a brief look at the working origins of these terms, which ought to clarify why we think like we do, and the thought processes of managers charged with applying the concepts. Linking engagement to discretionary effort, Towers Perrin note that 'another way to think about engagement is the extent to which employees put discretionary effort into their work, in the form of extra time, brainpower and energy'. This particular report concludes that discretionary effort is the endgame for effective engagement, and acknowledges that 'having a critical mass of employees who freely give that effort is of tremendous value' (2003, p.2). Taylor, associated with the theory of scientific management (Taylorism), viewed discretion largely in a negative light, arguing that if workers were relied upon to employ high levels of discretion, they would slow down productivity. His approach, which championed rigid supervisory regimes, suggested the removal of as much discretion as possible from work (at the time largely focused on production line activities in industrial America). In that period (the turn of the twentieth century) jobs with high levels of discretion were only associated with those who worked for themselves, such as farmers or highly skilled craftsmen. The wisdom of the day dictated that work ought to be oriented towards removing as much discretion as possible from the workplace, in an attempt to 'manage out' errors (*Poke Yoke* in Systems Thinking terms) and maximise productivity (Yankelovich and Immerwahr, 1984). Fast forward 100 years or so and the focus is now concerned with unlocking discretionary effort, largely through psychological constructs such as identity, commitment, control and motivation. However, there is caution: 'although improved performance and productivity is at the heart of engagement, it cannot be achieved by a mechanistic approach which tries to extract discretionary effort by manipulating employees' commitment and emotions' (MacLeod and Clarke, 2009, p.9). To conclude, we view discretion and discretionary effort in positive terms, but it is clearly not seen like this by all, and many command-and-control approaches still have Taylorism at their heart.

Creating the right environment for a workforce to experience meaning and purpose in their work is very often easier said than done, with a multitude of challenges and issues to deal with on a daily basis. These may range from supplier problems to customer complaints, but the binding phenomenon will often be how these groups of people feel about the way they have been treated. And we say feel because it may not be reality; the perception is often the thing that judgement is made upon. This can almost be to an extent where actually what is reality is either awful or fantastic. It is the way people feel that is often what is acted upon. This was probably best summed up by poet and civil rights activist Maya Angelou in her beautiful words (quoted in Rathus, 2012, p.246): 'I've learned that people will forget what you said, people will forget what you did, but people will never forget how you made them feel.' She herself was a superb example of personal resilience and we would recommend taking the time to look at her life history. Sadly, she died in 2014.

How people feel, how they perceive work and their approach are critical for well-being. Organisations, for all the right reasons, can do all the wrong things. Incentivising work is one such approach that can cause great angst and division in the workplace. It may not be badged as such; in some public sector organisations they call it reward and recognition. We would urge caution when setting up and embedding such schemes in the workplace. The unintended consequences can be quite damaging to staff. Monetary incentives are a good example. It seems that nobody really wants to reveal his or her own earnings, or bonuses. This leads to awkward conversations and feelings of envy or jealousy – and yet we take this and somehow believe that incentivising further will result in productivity. Employees already view salary points with great suspicion. Doing the same job as your co-worker and being paid more or less solely because of the number of years you have been at the firm always seems wrong, even though most public sector employers use this payment model. We do advocate reward by way of good management, for example being told you have done a great job, when deserved of course. This is another pitfall; inauthentic platitudes for the sake of it that nobody really believes can also be damaging. So, the rewards need to be authentic; otherwise the result will be the unintended consequence that workers, for example, may not feel valued, trusted or job secure.

Later in this book we will explore how organisations can gauge this 'feeling' by using effective survey instruments to measure the attitudes and perceptions of the workforce. This is particularly useful when conducting interventions, such as resilience training, to see if they have made any difference to the workforce or not. What is really interesting is the very low impact that features such as pay have on these feelings. Study after study places remuneration very low on the wellbeing scale, and although a component of job satisfaction, once wellbeing metrics are employed it features very low down, if at all. Features such as psychological safety, meaningful work, good leadership, security and good working relationships are high on the concern list for employees.

So what does the physical environment look like, tangibly? Are we talking about things such as Biophilia? Or is it the way things get done, or other cultural artefacts? Or is it a mixture of all these things? Let us spend a little time discussing some of the aspects of a fascinating concept known as Biophilia. It has been described as the 'innate tendency to focus on life and lifelike processes' by Edward Wilson (1984), who wrote an interesting book of the same name on the subject. So how does this relate to the workplace? The modern office space has changed dramatically over the years. The UK TV drama *Mr Selfridge* illustrated this very well, with the individual offices of the administration staff arranged along a dark wood-clad corridor, the innards masked by opaque glass and intricate lead beading. Now we see big open-plan office space. But which is better for the workforce? The open-space offices can be extremely noisy, and we would suggest are better suited to extroverts. Some proponents argue that the open office lends itself to greater collaboration and is better for camaraderie. Some commentators argue that it is less likely to lead to increased wellbeing and productivity and there is no privacy. We have reported previously on how open-plan offices can lead workers to perceive they are being treated as units of production, very much like a piece of office equipment, and as such can feel undervalued and experience low job satisfaction and decreased meaning and purpose. In the office environment, the notion of Biophilia involves the introduction of plant life into the workspace, good air quality in the office and having plenty of windows (natural light) for workers to look out onto natural scenes. Interestingly, views of busy roads seemingly have the opposite effect.

Aligning your leaders

Leadership plays such a huge part in the wellbeing landscape that it cannot be anything other than at the forefront of the minds of those charged with public services. The skills required to lead public services, as alluded to earlier, are very different from what they were just a few years ago. The pace and scale of change facing public service employees are unprecedented, and leaders need to be alert to the dynamic needs of their workforce. We simplified this in our model in Figure 3.1 as the ability to know enough about one's employees to notice when things are not right and to have the skills to intervene quickly and effectively. What we are saying here is that employers, managers, leaders and all those charged with people responsibility should be trained, educated and knowledgeable in dealing with people on an emotional level. Although sometimes referred to as 'soft skills', we would argue that these are amongst the most difficult tasks a modern day supervisor faces, and to be competent requires self-actualisation, sensitivity and attention. We were concerned about the small amount of management training in the public sector that had a focus on wellbeing, and the competency levels of leaders when dealing with wellbeing issues. Fundamentally, we would hope that this book goes some way to helping leaders both understand wellbeing and resilience and create workplace environments where employees can prosper and draw meaning and purpose from their everyday working life. They can feel secure, have a good work–life balance (or integration, as we would suggest), have good working relationships and generally feel they are leading a fulfilling and worthwhile life that contributes to society as a whole.

A simple way to consider effective leadership is by focusing on three aspects, which we have labelled here as 1) knowing your staff, 2) knowing your stuff and 3) knowing yourself. As depicted in Figure 3.3, these are interlinked, and we argue that all three elements are vital for successful workplace leadership outcomes. Taking a simple view of each of these in turn may be fruitful here. Whilst we do not wish to go into a journey of discovery, it is important to know how you yourself both operate and are viewed by those around you. Your own leadership style is something you need to be conscious of. How that style impacts on others is also critical for employee wellbeing. We all have a view of what good looks like, but it is important to keep in mind your overall effect. Knowing yourself can be the hardest part of this offering, but equally one that can yield the largest rewards, for you personally and for those around you. Knowing those around you can pay dividends too

FIGURE 3.3   A simple leadership model: knowing your stuff, staff and self

and can be increasingly challenging in the era of remote or virtual working, home working, flexible working and so on. Having a plan around workforce engagement is important here and can be key to followership. Equipping staff, trusting them, having strong relationships and the right attitude are all issues to consider. Finally we need to be operationally competent, which we have labelled 'knowing your stuff'. Being from the north of England, we thought this added a gritty edge to our model, à la Sean Bean! Sometimes this can be overlooked, in spite of the numerous pieces of research that tell us that the workforce consider it essential that leaders know about the work they are doing, and preferably have done it before themselves. We understand that, especially with the technical advancements being made, this is not always possible, but we would expect leaders to consider how they would feel about being led by somebody with no grasp at all of what their role entailed?

Discretionary effort

The term is used to describe the amount of effort people are prepared to give of themselves voluntarily. Known as extra-role effort in the US, it describes behaviours that cannot be prescribed or perhaps required, or that may run into trouble if pre-scribed, i.e. you will be nice to customers. It includes gestures, manners, niceties, common decency, loyalty (when nobody is looking!) and so on, such as looking after company equipment, being kind to colleagues, going the extra mile and so on. The reason it is so important in terms of leadership is that it is very often the leader or manager that inspires or motivates someone to give more of themselves than they are contracted to do, to be more positive in the workplace, be happier and so on. The immediate supervisor, according to Bateman and Organ (1983), represents the most direct source of variance in the exchange affect of discretionary effort, and thus they play a (if not the) crucial role. We highlight the positive importance also because public services, by their very nature, depend heavily on high levels of discretionary effort. Although we have touched on this in other parts of the book, we will explain the hypothesis behind our thinking here. Having a good understanding of this, in terms of management, will return you an increase in performance, and beyond.

Discretionary effort, we argue, can be as much as 50% of an employee's productivity. We suggest the terms performance and productivity can be interchanged for the benefit of this illustration, dependent on how service is viewed within a particular organisation. As we note, much of the work of public services is not involved in making a product, though there will be exceptions to this of course. What we suggest is that providing a service is not an easy notion to fully understand. What is a service? Who is the customer for each interchange? How do we know if the customers are satisfied with the service they receive? What is apparent is that it is beneficial if public service workers engage fully with their publics. We suggest that, in order to avoid burnout, a sustainable work rate may be 85%, basing this on operations management literature; see, for example, the Coping Zone (Johnston and Clark, 2008). When we now look at the minimum work effort required, that is just enough to stay out of trouble, avoid a sanction and so on, this, we hypothesise, could be as low as 35% (see Figure 3.4). This leaves 50% of what we are going to call, by way of illustrating the point, discretionary effort.

We know most of this effort is driven by the relationship an employee has with their employer, and studies have shown that leadership has a huge role to play in this; see, for example, our study of discretionary effort and engagement in policing (Hesketh et al., 2016). So what can leaders expect from this discretionary effort in terms of workers' productivity? In a longitudinal study in the US this effort consisted of helping co-workers with their work, keeping the workplace clean and tidy and free from physical dangers, enjoying good working relationships, and such (Bateman and Organ, 1983). Wiley (2009) suggests that as few as a third of workers are engaged in the UK. He claims that the leadership behaviours and practices can be very different in organisations seeking a high engagement workforce, evoking trust and confidence in senior leaders, which he argues leads to high performance as a direct consequence. He concedes this high performance is delivered, to a large extent, via discretionary effort. Also making links to engagement, the seminal work in the UK of MacLeod and Clarke (2009) on 'Engage for Success' noted that the focus is now on unlocking discretionary effort, largely through psychological constructs such as identity, commitment, control and motivation. The implication for managers who focus on high engagement, and are cognisant of the concept of discretionary effort, is that they can expect a high return on that focus. Together with employee wellbeing generally, these returns can be substantial in terms of performance and/or productivity, as well as improved working relationships. As a result of employing high levels of discretionary effort, managers will find that their people will be inspired and motivated to carry out their duties with meaning and purpose, resulting in sustainable high levels of quality and performance. We will look at meaning and purpose in ethics shortly, but a further consideration may be that as the nature of the modern workplace evolves, and knowledge workers move to more flexible, remote or virtual practices, the impact that discretionary effort has on the bottom line should not be overlooked or underestimated. Based on research relating to engagement, and linking the two concepts,

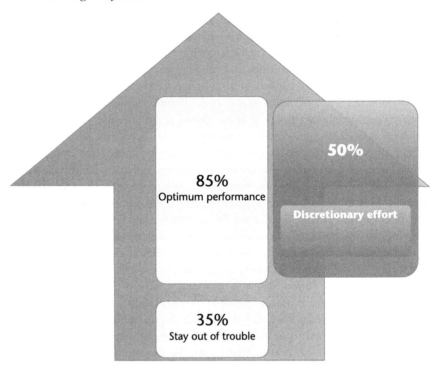

FIGURE 3.4   Hypothesis for discretionary effort

unlocking or realising this will deliver a high and sustainable return. In terms of adding public value, popularised by Hartley, Benington, Alford and Moore, it may also go some way to answering the questions posed earlier in this section.

Ethical leadership

When thinking about ethics and ethical behaviour, it is sometimes convenient to treat the subject as an aside, or a consideration. What we would argue is that ethics should be the staple of all wellbeing activity, thinking and creation. Ethics, or *moral philosophy*, is about right and wrong. Very rarely do we see any wellbeing as a wrong. As a branch of philosophy, ethics shares a great deal with wellbeing, its origins lying in the word *ethikos* – relating to one's character – and the word *ethos* – relating to habits and customs. Further linking to wellbeing, as a branch of philosophy ethics asks: what is the best way to live? This clearly resonates with questions about meaning and purpose in working life, which we often see in the wellbeing narrative. Larry Churchill asked us to think critically about moral value, again forging links with the wider wellbeing debate. It is incredibly important to ensure that employees have an understanding of their personal values and beliefs, and that the organisation realises how leaders within it influence the development of an ethical organisational culture. The strategic importance of strong ethical leadership cannot be underestimated, and the role of the leader is paramount to success. Organisations that promote ethical behaviour, prevent wrongdoing and have effective whistleblowing processes will undoubtedly create a workplace environment that is far more congruent with workplace wellbeing than those that do not. Research has also shown that fairness, respect and ethical behaviour have a positive impact on the public. We also know that fairness shapes the attitudes of employees, and that fairness also exceeds the expectations of most employees and can impact positively on productivity. Ethics and fairness are also 'teachable', and research suggests that organisations that do not conscientiously promote ethical behaviour have higher rates of sickness absence, presenteeism and general workplace disengagement. The literature on Organisational Justice and Procedural Fairness is quick to highlight this (Bradford et al., 2014).

Collective leadership

The notion of collective leadership first arose in comparisons with communism and the distributed style that emerged from that approach. Latterly, commentators have seen its worth when considering how much information is pouring into an organisation, and how leaders in that organisation manage it. There appears to be a consensus that there is too much for one person, or even a few people, to absorb, interpret and action in any meaningful way. Therefore, a collective approach is called for. In public services this may cause issues for the traditionally embedded heroic leadership styles that have adorned the corridors of power in days gone by. Here we instantly pick up on two very different approaches to leadership, one that is highly consensual and one that is very much command and control. To be clear, we suggest the latter cannot exist alongside authentic employee wellbeing and engagement approaches. We also suggest that it does not sit alongside leadership ethics and principles of ethical working life, as suggested by Nolan. Therefore, moves towards collective leadership approaches are a big deal for public services and impact significantly on the workforce wellbeing landscape. This new approach to 'power sharing' may be very difficult for some to consume, while to others it may be a case of 'about time'! We see these approaches playing out where areas of expertise in a particular area are called for and, grade aside, the best person for that business area makes the decision based on the evidence they have been educated or trained in or have subject expertise in. And what is more, the rest of the organisation will follow them, will trust them and will support their decisions. Followership is a key area of collective leadership. A further key area is the culture and engagement that need to accompany collective leadership. With origins in a supportive mindset, or growth mindset, it is easy to see the shift that may be required by some. However, this approach can provide huge rewards, for example by distributing work more evenly across an organisation, avoiding situations in which some have too much and some have too little. It is easy to draw in where the ethical components of working life now come into play. Collective leadership assumes a positive operating climate, which we know is beneficial to workforce wellbeing. If we take the moral philosophy high ground here, or the way we live our life, it is straightforward to connect the dots. One of the underpinning ethical constructs is that of trust, and leadership styles that invite openness and honesty as critical components evoke the trust of the workforce and lead to a far more conducive working environment, as we have mentioned in previous chapters. This also facilitates visioning and strategy communications in a far more coherent manner, listening and including employee voice. And whilst we are on an ethical vein, it is clear to see how notions of fairness and transparency are dealt with also. These strong ethical values really form the backbone of collective leadership, as well as dealing with the new working environment that many are faced with, as discussed earlier. Having the organisational maturity to create an environment in which employees can be involved in all aspects of the business, have a voice and are actively engaged in the success of the organisation, whatever that entails, seems to us at least to be the way forward.

References

(All website URLs were accessed on 6 June 2017.)

Bakker, A. and Demerouti, E. (2008) 'Towards a Model of Work Engagement', *Career Development International*, 13(3), pp. 209–223.

Bateman, T. and Organ, D. (1983) 'Job Satisfaction and the Good Soldier: The Relationship between Affect and Employee "Citizenship"', *Academy of Management Journal (pre-1986)*, 26(4), p. 587.

BBC (2017) 'Simon Wessely on Unexplained Medical Syndromes'. In: Wessely, S. (ed.) *The Life Scientific*. London: BBC.

Bradford, B., Quinton, P., Myhill, A. and Porter, G. (2014) 'Why Do "the Law" Comply? Procedural Justice, Group Identification and Officer Motivation in Police Organizations', *European Journal of Criminology*, 11(1), pp. 110–131.

Cooper, C. L. (2004) *Stress: A Brief History*. Malden, MA: Blackwell.

Cooper, C. L. and Cartwright, S. (1997) 'An Intervention Strategy for Workplace Stress', *Journal of Psychosomatic Research*, 43(1), pp. 7–16.

Cornum, R. (2012) *Can We Teach Resilience?* Available from The Young Foundation.

Crawford, E. R., Lepine, J. A. and Rich, B. L. (2010) 'Linking Job Demands and Resources to Employee Engagement and Burnout: A Theoretical Extension and Meta-Analytic Test', *Journal of Applied Psychology*, 95(5), pp. 834–848.

Diener, E. (2000) 'Subjective Well-Being: The Science of Happiness and a Proposal for a National Index', *American Psychologist*, 55(1), p. 34.

Gayton, S. D. and Lovell, G. P. (2012) 'Resilience in Ambulance Service Paramedics and Its Relationships with Well-Being and General Health', *Traumatology*, 18(1), pp. 58–64.

Gerich, J. (2015) 'Leaveism and Illness-Related Behaviour', *Occupational Medicine*, 65(9), pp. 746–752.

Grant, L. and Kinman, G. (2013) 'Bouncing Back? Personal Representations of Resilience of Student and Experienced Social Workers', *Social Work in Action*, 25(5), pp. 349–366.

Haglund, M. E. M., Nestadt, P. S., Cooper, N. S., Southwick, S. M. and Charney, D. S. (2007) 'Psychobiological Mechanisms of Resilience: Relevance to Prevention and Treatment of Stress-Related Psychopathology', *Development and Psychopathology*, 19(3), pp. 889–920.

Hesketh, I. and Cooper, C. (2014) 'Leaveism at Work', *Occupational Medicine*, 64(3), pp. 146–147.

Hesketh, I., Smith, J. and Ivy, J. (2014b) 'Keeping the Peelian Spirit: Resilience and Spirituality in Policing', *Police Journal: Theory, Practice and Principles*, 87(3), pp. 154–166.

Hesketh, I., Cooper, C. and Ivy, J. (2015b) 'Leaveism and Work–Life Integration: The Thinning Blue Line?', *Policing*, 9(2), pp. 183–194.

Hesketh, I., Cooper, C. and Ivy, J. (2016) 'Wellbeing and Engagement in Policing: The Key to Unlocking Discretionary Effort', *Policing*, pp. 1–12.

Johns, G. (2010) 'Presenteeism in the Workplace: A Review and Research Agenda', *Journal of Organizational Behavior*, 31(4), pp. 519–542.

Johnston, R. and Clark, G. (2008) *Service Operations Management*, 3rd edn. London: Pearson Education.

Luthans, F. (2002) 'The Need for and Meaning of Positive Organizational Behavior', *Journal of Organizational Behavior*, 23(6), pp. 695–706.

MacLeod, D. and Clarke, N. (2009) *Engaging for Success: Enhancing Performance through Employee Engagement*. Department for Business Innovation and Skills. Available at: www.bis.gov.uk/files/file52215.pdf.

Mallack, L. (1998) 'Measuring Resilience in Health Care Provider Organizations', *Health Manpower Management*, 24(4), pp. 148–152.

Masten, A. S. (2014) 'Global Perspectives on Resilience in Children and Youth', *Child Development*, 85(1), pp. 6–20.

Palmer, S. and Cooper, C. L. (2010) *How to Deal with Stress*, 2nd edn. London: Kogan Page.

Paton, D. (2006) 'Critical Incident Stress Risk in Police Officers: Managing Resilience and Vulnerability', *Traumatology*, 12(3), pp. 198–206.

Rathus, S. A. (2012) *Psychology: Concepts and Connections*, 10th edn. Belmont, CA: Wadsworth.

Rayton, B., Dodge, T. and D'Aneleze, G. (2012) *Engage for Success: The Evidence*. London. Available at: http://opus.bath.ac.uk/35611/1/.

Robertson, I. and Cooper, C. (2010) 'Full Engagement: The Integration of Employee Engagement and Psychological Well-Being', *Leadership and Organization Development Journal*, 31(4), pp. 324–336.

Schaufeli, W. and Bakker, A. B. (2004) 'Job Demands, Job Resources, and Their Relationship with Burnout and Engagement: A Multi-sample Study', *Journal of Organizational Behavior*, 25, pp. 293–315.

Schaufeli, W., Salanova, B., González-romá, M., Bakker, V., Bakker, A. and Bakker, B. (2002) 'The Measurement of Engagement and Burnout: A Two Sample Confirmatory Factor Analytic Approach', *Journal of Happiness Studies*, 3(1), pp. 71–92.

Seligman, M. (2003) *Authentic Happiness: Using the New Positive Psychology to Realize Your Potential for Deep Fulfillment*. London: Nicholas Brealey Publishing.

Seligman, M. (2011) *Flourish: A New Understanding of Happiness and Well-Being – and How to Achieve Them*. London: Nicholas Brealey Publishing.

Selye, H. (1984) *The Stress of Life*. New York: McGraw-Hill.

Southwick, S. and Charney, D. (2012b) 'The Science of Resilience: Implications for the Prevention and Treatment of Depression', *Science*, 338(6103), pp. 79–82.

Suadicani, P., Olesen, K., Bonde, J. and Gyntelberg, F. (2014) 'Psychosocial Work Conditions Associated with Sickness Absence among Hospital Employees', *Occupational Medicine*, 64(7), pp. 503–508.

Viner, R. (1999) 'Putting Stress in Life: Hans Selye and the Making of Stress Theory', *Social Studies of Science*, 29(3), pp. 391–410.

Wiley, J. (2009) *Driving Success through Performance Excellence and Employee Engagement*. Online: Kenexa Research Institute. Available at: www.academia.edu/4438802/Driving_Success_Through_PE_and_EE.

Wilson, E. O. (1984) *Biophilia*. Cambridge, MA: Harvard University Press.

Yankelovich, D. and Immerwahr, J. (1984) 'Putting the Work Ethic to Work', *Society*, 21(2), pp. 58–76.

Yerkes, R. and Dodson, J. (1908) 'The Relation of Strength of Stimulus to Rapidity of Habit-Formation', *Journal of Comparative Neurology and Psychology*, 18(1), pp. 459–482.

Zander, M., Hutton, A. and King, L. (2013) 'Exploring Resilience in Paediatric Oncology Nursing Staff', *Collegian*, 20(1), pp. 17–25.

3 The future of work – talent required

*Maggi Evans, John Arnold,
and Andrew Rothwell*

Introduction

The changing workplace is a topic that interests people across many fields. Our intention here is not to compete with the excellent work of others, but to provide a summary of some of the themes that emerge across these varied sources. Footnotes will guide you to the source documents if you want to find out more. For this summary we've identified five key themes: the macrostructure of organisations; the internal structure of organisations; demographic changes; technological opportunities; and changes in career paths. In discussing these, we want to stress that we are describing them separately because it helps with presenting the information and thinking it through. However, as shown in Figure 2.1, the five themes inevitably interact such that changes in demography influence changes in structure and technology, changes in technology also influence changes in structures, and, in turn, changes in structures influence changes in technology. Similarly there are interactions between people's career paths and career expectations and the opportunities that are available to them as a result of macrostructures, internal structures, demographics and technology. In turn, the careers people want will create different resource opportunities and challenges for organisations.

Given that talent management is a strategic activity with largely long-term rather than short-term payback, it is essential that it is positioned in the context of the next wave of change. Therefore, having explored key trends and predictions for each theme, we then consider the implications of this for talent and career. This helps to establish how well the current talent models and approaches will adapt to these possible changes and help to drive competitive advantage. As you will see, our conclusion is that the current interpretation and implementation of talent management is ill-equipped to meet future needs as it is based on a set of assumptions about the workplace that seem to be no longer appropriate.

Predictions for the future of work

Macrostructure of organisations

We have borrowed the term *macrostructure* from sociology. It's a broad term that refers to the way society (or in our case, organisations across sectors and geographies) is structured in terms of relationships, dependencies and properties.

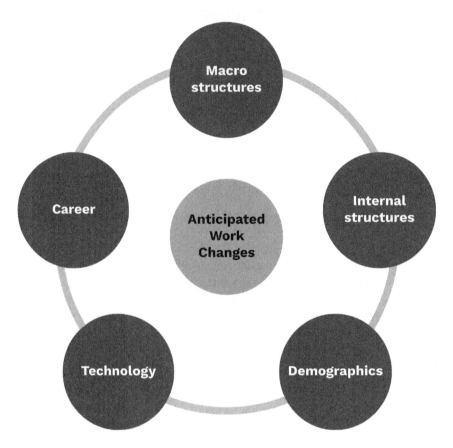

Figure 2.1 Anticipated workplace changes

The second half of the twentieth century and the early part of the twenty-first have seen ongoing amalgamation of businesses and domination by a few big players (think Google, Amazon, Netflix, 3M or General Electric). In the West, there has been growth in office-based work, service and distribution roles and a decline of roles in goods production. According to one recent report, added value service-based roles now make up nearly 80% of the US economy, with exports growing faster than any other sector.[1] However, in the midst of this growth of large business, new business models are emerging, which could provide insight into future changes.

Some of these new business models are based on facilitating direct contact between the service user and the service provider, sometimes referred to as the 'human cloud'[2] (e.g. Uber, fiverr, upwork, Airbnb and crowdsourcing platforms). They provide the flexibility that many organisations and individuals want to enable them to respond quickly to changing demands. Accurately understanding the growth in this type of organisational structure is difficult – by the nature of these businesses they don't publish annual reports for us to analyse. However, most would agree that the so-called 'gig economy' and the number of micro-enterprises are growing,[3] and some researchers predict that this will continue to grow, leading to a much smaller proportion of workers who will operate as employees with long-term, secure contracts.[4] This employment change represents a radical shift in the relationship between the employer and the worker. The psychological contract is fundamentally redrawn as the worker accepts less security and rights and accepts greater responsibility for keeping skills up-to-date and relevant. Similarly, it creates smaller discrete packages of work conducted by individuals who may not have any interest in the wider aims of the organisation they are working on behalf of. These individuals may be essential to the success of the organisation, or they may hold vital information, relationships and knowledge. But as things stand, some of them will not form part of the population that is included within the remit of talent management.

Another potential change has been described as new 'ecosystems'[5] of specialist smaller businesses which emerge to provide the services and products that the large corporations find difficult to deliver. These may involve collaborations and alliances between a large number of niche organisations or individuals, each at the cutting edge of their field. These smaller, highly focused, entrepreneurial organisations provide a very different employment deal to their workers, often based on highly flexible ways of working and the opportunity to be involved in cutting-edge projects. This approach is already operating in some sectors, for example, crowdsourcing labs and the successful Procter & Gamble 'Connect + Develop'[6] initiative. This sources innovation partners rather than relying on the traditional model of internal (or fully acquired) research and development. Again, such business models leave bigger organisations relying on the expertise of talented people who lie outside its traditional organisational boundaries.

For talent management, this has wide-ranging implications. As indicated earlier, these changes challenge the typical boundaries of talent management, with strategically important people in strategically important roles situated outside the organisation. This requires consideration of the ways to interact and work together, for example, in terms of ongoing skills development and loyalty. It also requires a review of talent practices and how they should be adapted to apply to people who are not directly employed by the organisation.

Internal structures of organisations

Internal structures of organisations are continually evolving as leaders try to respond better to customer needs, to increase efficiency or to exploit new opportunities. As well as adapting the patterns and the boxes of reporting lines and roles, they also look at how to adapt the formal rules, processes, power, behaviours and sometimes the informal ones too. Over the years there have been different trends and solutions. There have been cycles of centralisation and decentralisation, of in-sourcing and outsourcing. Most organisations now operate a form of matrix management to try to achieve the best of both worlds, with individual roles being clearly defined to support performance management, but also using dotted lines to encourage collaboration across functional and business unit lines. However, many structures still largely resemble a traditional hierarchy. Some claim that it is now time to challenge these structures and we now need to redefine the way in which people work together to achieve a common aim.

Many of the ideas for change stem from the application of complexity theory.[7] This encourages us to change our view of an organisation. Instead of seeing it as a machine to be managed and controlled, we are presented with the organisation as a complex adaptive system – one that, like the human brain or the internet, can manage itself without the need for hierarchy and one point of control. Over the years there have been examples of large and successful organisations turning their back on traditional hierarchies and finding new ways of doing things, for instance, Ricardo Semler's story of transforming the fortunes of Semco,[8] his family manufacturing business. The approach was radical. There were no set work hours, all employees voted on important decisions, people were encouraged to take a sabbatical to learn new skills, many employees set their own pay, there were few policies, and all corporate information was transparently shared with everyone.

More recently, Frederic Laloux[9] linked the evolution of organisations with advanced psychological development, describing different organisational structures by colours. Traditional organisations are termed as amber, with a focus on conforming. More developed organisations are categorised as orange (achievement) and then green (pluralistic). The most developed organisation is described as teal, with a clear purpose, the ability to self-organise and a safe space where people can connect and bring their whole self to work. Similarly, Mercer[10] describes these as 'molten structures', a way to respond to the need for plasticity with ongoing flattening and increasing emphasis on building networked communities (both internal and external). Some of these ideas are very radical and difficult to envisage, but there is growing interest.

Many of the principles of complexity and teal are recognised as a way in which organisations can achieve competitive advantage and be ready to respond quickly as the macrostructures around them change. Some of the principal differences of such an approach were summarised by Deloitte in their 2017 report on Global Human Capital Trends (see Table 2.1)[11] (Rewriting the rules for the digital age).

In our experience, many of these ideas are still at the experimental stage. However, we increasingly work with leaders who are interested in developing this thinking and already experimenting with parts of it. For example, project-based structures, offices designed to promote conversation and collaboration, organisations offering a variety of work contracts and processes based on conversation rather than documentation. For these organisations, such new approaches create a need for a fundamentally different approach to talent management. As the organising principles shift from defined roles to projects, succession planning takes a different form and becomes more about deployment of skills than job title. As the work environment creates ongoing change, the nature, opportunities and purpose of personal development changes. As the role

Table 2.1 Deloitte summary of old rules and new rules for work

Old rules	New rules
Organised for efficiency and effectiveness	Organised for learning, innovation and customer impact
Company viewed as a hierarchy, with hierarchical decision rights, structure and leadership progression	Company viewed as an agile network, empowered by team leaders and fuelled by collaboration and knowledge-sharing
Structure based on business function with functional leaders and global functional groups	Structure based on work and projects, with teams focused on products, customers and services
Advancement through promotion upward with many levels to progress through	Advancement through many assignments, diverse experiences and multifunctional leadership assignments
People "become leaders" through promotion	People "create followers" to grow in influence and authority
Lead by direction	Lead by orchestration
Culture ruled by fear of failure and perceptions of others	Culture of safety, abundance and importance of risk-taking and innovation
Rules-based	Playbook-based
Roles and job titles clearly defined	Teams and responsibilities clearly defined, but roles and job titles change regularly
Process-based	Project-based

Source: Reproduced with permission: Josh Bersin, Bill Pelster, Jeff Schwarz, and Bernard Van der Vyver, "Introduction: Rewriting the rules for the digital age", *2017 Deloitte Global Human Capital Trends*, Deloitte Insights, February 28, 2017.

of the leader evolves, the skills, experiences and motivations of successful leaders will be different, requiring leaders who can rapidly help new teams to form and perform, who can bring out the best in people whatever the nature and form of their working relationship.

Demographic changes

According to an OECD report, projections for Japan illustrate the scale of the problem of falling birth-rates and aging population.[12] The Japanese government expects the country's overall population to decrease by 22–23% between 2010 and 2050, with people 65+ years accounting for 40% of the total. The 'elderly dependency ratio' (proportion of people aged 65+ to proportion of working-age people) is a particular concern and has risen across OECD countries in recent decades. This is likely to increase further as a result of longer lives. Alongside this is concern regarding population growth in developing nations. This is well illustrated by comparing the dependency ratio of Japan (45 in 2017) with that of India, a high growth nation (9 in 2017).[13] However, in line with trends observed as other nations develop, the rate of population growth in developing countries is declining as health, living conditions and education improvements are reflected in lower birth rates. For countries experiencing a declining population, the key challenges are to increase productivity, increase participation in the workplace beyond 65, encourage immigration of workers from other countries and find sustainable ways to fund and support older people. For the still-growing nations, the challenge is to increase education, job creation and political stability. For individuals worldwide, there are also significant questions about how to fund later life and the challenge of reconciling work–ability (literally the ability to do work) with increased life expectancy.[14]

All of these changes have a significant impact on the composition of the future workforce and therefore on the available talent. There are three particular issues we will briefly explore here: globalisation of the employment market, increasing work participation and generational differences. Increasing productivity offers additional ways to respond to changing demographics, but these will be explored alongside technical solutions later.

One response to these demographic changes is to see the workforce as global. This is already happening as organisations look to transfer work to places where there is a higher availability of qualified workers (with associated lower costs). Having started as 'off-shoring' (often in Asia or Eastern Europe), many organisations have reaped huge financial and talent benefits from broadening their talent market in these ways.[15] Growth in the availability of talented people from these locations is likely to continue, as illustrated by the statistic that if current trends continue, then by the 2020s, 40% of all young people with a degree will come from China and India.[16] Within many organisations there are also increasing efforts to look at resourcing requirements and deployment through a global rather than local lens. For example, if there is a need for a specialist skill, that skill can be searched for across the organisation rather than just within the local business unit or geography. Such a global resourcing model creates an internal job market place with an acceptance that the skills can lie anywhere in the organisation and virtual teams are an appropriate delivery mechanism. The global skills and talent challenge is complex and paradoxical. On one hand, there is the global phenomenon of graduate underemployment. On the other hand, there is the repeated complaint from business that there is a shortage of suitable individuals for leadership positions and a shortage of technological talent. Many countries wish to reduce the reliance on expatriates to fill senior positions and develop more 'local' talent. Meanwhile, other countries experience 'brain drain' as highly educated individuals seek more lucrative positions overseas. Nevertheless the global homogeneity of business systems, the prevalence of English as a global business language and rising education levels have caused a radical shift. Jobs in the so-called 'knowledge based economy' are moving to where labour costs are lower. In organisational talent terms, this can create challenges in global succession planning and the development of professional skills.[17]

Demographic changes are also stimulating us to rethink what we mean by our 'working life'. In many countries, government policy is contributing to this as state retirement ages increase in response to unsustainable financial models of state retirement benefits, with the consequence that working lives become longer. Many of these issues are brought together in a fascinating book by Lynda Gratton and Andrew Scott of London Business School.[18] They suggest that these demographic changes require us to shift our mindset of the normal stages of life. For generations, the expectation has been three key stages: education, work and retirement. However, with a longer, healthier life and smaller working population, we will need to think more in terms of multiple cycles of education, work and other things (which may include greater leisure or caring or community-based work). For the workplace this necessitates a significant change in how we think about career, engagement and the relationship between age and seniority. For example, it could be that apprentices in their 50s train alongside those in their 20s. We need to think how to motivate and engage people over a working life that extends into their 70s. Equally it creates opportunities for new approaches to remuneration, for example, the opportunity to fund a 'learning pot' rather than a 'pension pot', as has been the case in Singapore with 'Skillsfuture'.[19]

Further workplace challenges could result from what are believed to be differences in motivations of the millennial generation. It is often suggested that millennials are looking for a different career deal, expecting a greater sense of purpose, a desire for learning, treatment as an individual, more rapid progression and regular positive reinforcement or feedback.[20] However, research evidence to support this is modest, and perhaps the biggest message here is the desire for individual treatment and meaning, which would seem to be increasingly valued by people of all generations.[21]

Technological opportunities

We are all aware that technology is dramatically changing the way we work, often referred to as the 'Fourth Industrial Revolution'.[22] To repeat the much quoted phrase from *Shift Happens*,[23] 'we are currently preparing students for jobs that don't yet exist, using technologies that haven't been invented, in order to solve problems we don't yet realise are problems'. More specific data also reinforce this view. For example, by 2020, smart cities will include 9.7 billion connected things, an increase from 1.1 billion in 2015, and driverless cars could free up 50 billion hours each year in the United States (a potential employment issue given that 40% of US males are currently employed in driving-based occupations).[24] There are bound to be many consequences of technological change, some bringing considerable ethical considerations. Rather than taking a broad look at these implications, in this section we will focus on two areas of particular relevance for the talent agenda: firstly the impact of technology on the skills that are needed and secondly the workplace opportunities arising from technology in terms of learning, collaboration and engagement.

The impact of technology on the nature of jobs is likely to be driven by the uptake of new technologies. A 2018 paper by PwC[25] suggests three waves of automation. Wave one, the algorithmic wave (to the early 2020s) is predicted to be largely about automation of processes and analysis of structured data.

This is anticipated to impact most on data-driven sectors including financial services. The second wave (to the late 2020s) is seen as being dominated by augmentation, with greater use of technology to support decision making and increased use in moving objects from place to place (such as in warehouses and airports). The third wave is seen as the autonomous wave (to the mid-2030s) with technological advances meaning that jobs requiring physical dexterity can be completed through robotics and that AI can take over problem-solving tasks in more complex situations.

The human impact of such advances were reviewed in a report commissioned by the UK's CIPD (Chartered Institute of Personnel and Development, the professional body for HR),[26] who concluded that technology would complement human skills, potentially removing mundane aspects of roles to enable more 'human work' and emotional interaction to take place. The view that 'human skills' will remain in demand is supported by the Mercer 2018 study on Global Talent Trends. Thus, in talent terms, we need to consider where human skills will add unique value that cannot readily be replicated by technology. These are the skills we will particularly need in our organisations of the future.

A second skill impact of technological advances is also made by both the CIPD research and the Mercer 2018 study. For these technologies to be developed and implemented, workers with deep technological expertise will be required. Workers who can rapidly adapt and learn new technologies and find ways to exploit them will be needed. Equally, all workers will need to be skilled at working with new and evolving technologies. Without this, uptake of technological solutions is likely to be hindered. In the context of talent, these points challenge both the roles people do and our current way of assessing people. For example, the HR function will need to be redefined as the compliance aspects of the work become increasingly automated. In recruitment, expecting a certain number of years' experience may no longer be relevant due to the decreasing half-life of technology and knowledge. Rather, the key skill will be the ability to learn, adapt and harness the power of a range of new technologies and to use them legally and ethically. These changes will apply to all people working with the organisation, be they employed or contracted, and in any of the four talent quadrants.

In addition to changing the nature of jobs and skills requirements, technology is likely to have a growing impact on learning, assessment and engagement. Comprehensive learning management systems (LMS) are now starting to realise the dreams of the early e-learning pioneers as bite-sized, relevant learning becomes available to employees via mobile, interactive apps.[27] Learning is also increasingly accessible with Massive Open On-line Courses (MOOCs) expanding (according to some data having over 80 million students enrolled)[28] and world-class events available to watch via TED talks and YouTube. This creates both benefits and challenges as employers try to understand the comparative value of traditional learning, MOOCs and self-learning. Technology has a role to play in assessment with increasing use of online and innovative tools such as gamification, AI evaluation of interview data and e-tray exercises.[29] Social media are also increasingly being used to reinforce employee branding as a tool to attract and engage talented employees. Utilising models and techniques from product marketing, such approaches are becoming progressively more sophisticated, especially to attract 'passive' candidates who are not actively job hunting.[30] Technological advances also make it easier to achieve the global collaboration that was explored as part of the changing macro and internal structures. For example, LinkedIn supports leaders and organisations in quickly identifying internal or external candidates with the skills or experience being sought.

All of these aspects of technology are likely to influence the future of talent management. Technological advances will create demand for different skills and experiences. They will also create opportunities for new ways of delivering the talent agenda.

Changes in career paths

Career is a commonly used term, often applied in quite a narrow way, traditionally referring to someone's hierarchical progression within a particular profession. However, within the academic literature, career is considered in broader terms as the way work is experienced over the course of a working life.[31] This relates not just to objective measures of career success (such as job title, salary and promotion history) but also to subjective measures (such as satisfaction, meaning and thriving).[32] Taking this wider description of career, it is easy to see how the structural, technological and demographic changes described earlier will create some fundamental changes in the way careers are experienced. Indeed changes in career have long been heralded with talk of the death of organisational careers, with people freely moving between roles.[33] In this section we explore two additional themes that are pertinent to talent and career: what people want from their career and the role of career self-management.

Will changes in the nature of work change what people want from their career? Research to date has suggested that despite the changing structures of employment, most people continue to think of careers as organisationally based.[34] Some suggest that new forms of career are now possible, combining some of the freedom, flexibility and empowerment of an individually driven career with the benefits of continuity, meaning and relationships that can emerge from being part of an organisation.[35] Others have taken this further, indicating that there needs to be a fundamental shift in the employee value proposition:[36] It is suggested that this needs to move from a loyalty or engagement contract to a 'thrive contract'. This moves attention from meeting the employee's needs for achievement, relationships and fairness to an environment that prioritises purpose, meaning and impact with joint career ownership and ongoing learning. This was summarised in a recent PwC report as the importance of helping people to thrive in order to deliver strong business performance.[37] They proposed that organisations need to focus more on the employee experience and embrace modern career paths that provide multiple routes to meet diverse individual needs (rather than the historic 'up or out' mindset). Common to much of the thinking on the future of career is the need to individualise, to recognise that people have different wants, needs and aspirations at different stages in their working lives. However, it may be naïve to have such aspirations for the development of thriving at work. A recent book by David Graeber[38] suggests that half of all jobs are pointless, and the proportion seems to be increasing. This creates inefficiency for the organisations and has a damaging psychological impact on people doing jobs that they can see are meaningless.

The second theme that emerges in career is the increasing focus on the individual as responsible for 'owning' their career. Our research shows that the idea of individual accountability is widely accepted by HR leaders and individuals. However, many people report that they don't know what this means in practice or how they can be proactive in developing their career within their own work context. Whilst some organisations are helping them (see Chapter 5 for examples), there tends to be a lack of information and support. The need for comprehensive information and support is also recognised by governments and policy makers who are keen to support individuals to be able to proactively manage their careers.[39] This is likely to become increasingly important with the work changes described earlier. There is a particular risk that people with low social capital[40] could find it difficult to find employment without career management skills. Indeed the European-funded ACUMEN project[41] has emphasised the importance of career management skills by describing them as the 'new literacy'.

Implications of these changes for talent management

The previous sections have, we hope, provided a helpful overview of some current and anticipated changes in the world of work. Many of the points we have raised will have significant implications for talent management. We have signposted some of these along the way and have now summarised them in Table 2.2.

Table 2.2 Implications of work changes for talent management

Change	Potential implications for talent management
Macrostructures	• Strategically critical skills and knowledge may lie outside organisational boundaries but need to be considered as part of the talent strategy. • Changes in the psychological contract are likely to impact on mutual commitment between employer and employee; established ways to engage and develop talented people will need to be reviewed. • Historical talent management success measures such as succession planning, retention, engagement, internal development and promotions may no longer be appropriate.

(Continued)

Table 2.2 (Continued)

Change	Potential implications for talent management
Internal structures	• Larger organisations will have a myriad of possible career pathways as there are fewer hierarchies and more project-based work; career development will need to be reappraised. • Global resourcing models make geographic location less relevant for larger organisations and open new opportunities for smaller organisations to consider. • Lifelong learning will have increasing importance, and learning agility will become a key capability, as does the ability to effectively collaborate, indicating new selection, development and performance management criteria.
Technical opportunities	• New specialisms will quickly evolve and command high market demand/price; organisations with access to these skills are likely to have competitive advantage, so early identification of needs and development of skills will become more critical. • Many businesses will depend on quick adoption, so workers who can quickly adapt and implement new technology will be in demand. • Joined-up thinking will be required with governments and educators in respect of skills and developing future labour supply and accessible retraining. • Technology will provide new opportunities for learning, attraction and engagement, but will require ongoing investment.
Demographic	• Generational integration will occur as people go through career stages at different ages and may require a change in expectations and selection criteria for different roles (such as apprenticeships). • Longer working life indicates a need to find ways to fund learning and retraining throughout employment. • Changes in geographical availability of talent with possible rising costs in developing markets suggest a need to constantly review availability and location of people with different skills.
Career pathways	• Increase in career self-management may disadvantage some people. Organisations may benefit from supporting individuals to manage their employability and career transitions. • Changing perceptions of career suggests the importance of understanding what our talented workers want from their work and providing greater flexibility. • Variety of career opportunities indicates the importance of developing new relationships with all workers (employees or others engaged in strategically important work), offering a clear employer value proposition and moving towards thriving.

Our summary indicates that it is time to reflect on talent management and how the approach may need to evolve to meet these predicted changes. When this is combined with the concerns raised in the previous chapter, the case for change becomes even more compelling. The previous predictions suggest that if we retain our current approaches, the scarcity mindset will be reinforced as the availability of 'ready now' 'traditionally employed' talent is likely to reduce. The changes also indicate that reliance on individual heroes will impede an organisation's ability to evolve and harness the power of self-managed teams. A dependence on formal process is also likely to reduce the ability to flex and quickly address emerging talent needs in innovative ways that respond to unique circumstances. Similarly, anchoring talent processes in historic assessments of what is needed is unlikely to deliver competitive advantage. Finally the future of work clearly suggests the need to respond to what the individual wants and to find a way to work in partnership, helping people to thrive and find the motivation which will drive their talent.

Reflections

In this chapter, we have introduced five themes to explore how the world of work seems to be changing. We have illustrated how these are likely to impact on the way talent management is approached if organisations want to retain competitive advantage. We have shown how these themes could magnify some of the challenges of talent management which we introduced in Chapter 1. This substantiates our view that talent management as it is currently practised is not fit for purpose in the short term and is likely to become even less effective in the future.

You may find the following questions helpful as you reflect on how changes in the workplace may impact on your future talent needs.

- What work changes have you observed over the past five years?
- What changes do you anticipate over the next five years?
- How could the changes in macrostructures change the key functions carried out by your organisation?
- What are the likely and possible changes to internal structures?
- Which demographic trends are most likely to impact your business in the next five years?
- What technical changes do you anticipate, and what are the hard-to-replicate 'human' skills that you may need?
- How do you think the requirements and expectations of the people who work in your organisation will change?
- How do you see these things impacting on your talent needs?
- Who else in your organisation is thinking about these implications?

Notes

1 Deloitte report https://www2.deloitte.com/content/dam/insights/us/articles/4674_IbtN-July-2018/DI_IbtN-July-2018.pdf (accessed 13.06.2019).

2 For example, see Schwab, K., 2017. *The fourth industrial revolution.* London: Penguin Random House.

3 Information from the Gig Economy Data Hub, a partnership between the ILR School at Cornell University and the Future of Work Initiative, www.gigeconomydata.org/ (accessed 13.06.2019). We are also aware that some of these changes have consistently been predicted for the past thirty years and have yet to materialise to the extent that was anticipated.

4 E.g. UK Commission for Employment and Skills report 'The Future of Work Jobs and Skills in 2030 https://assets.publishing.service.gov.uk/government/uploads/system/uploads/attachment_data/file/303335/the_future_of_work_key_findings_edit.pdf (accessed 13.06.2019).

5 Gratton, L and Scott, A., 2016. *The 100 year Life: Living and working in an age of longevity.* London: Bloomsbury.

6 www.pgconnectdevelop.com/what-is-connect-develop/ (accessed 13.06.2019).

7 For a short introduction to complexity theory, we suggest the following video www.youtube.com/watch?v=i-ladOjo1QA (accessed 28.06.2019).

8 See Semler, R., 1993. *Maverick.* New York: Warner Books.

9 Laloux, F., 2014. *Reinventing organizations: A guide to creating organizations inspired by the next stage in human consciousness.* Nelson Parker.

10 www.mercer.com/our-thinking/career/voice-on-talent/people-first-mercers-2018-global-talent-trends-study.html (accessed 28.06.2018).

11 Deloitte in their 2017 report on Global Human Capital Trends (Rewriting the rules for the digital age), https://www2.deloitte.com/cn/en/pages/human-capital/articles/global-human-capital-trends-2017.html (accessed 13.06.2019).

12 http://oecdinsights.org/2016/04/11/the-case-of-the-shrinking-country-japans-demographic-and-policy-challenges-in-5-charts/ shows the particular challenges facing Japan and suggests that Japan illustrates the problems that will be faced by other OECD countries in future years (accessed 13.06.2019).

13 For a full list by nation, visit https://data.worldbank.org/indicator/SP.POP.DPND.OL (accessed 13.06.2019).

14 For some early research on this, see Nielsen, J., 1999. Employability and workability among Danish employees. *Experimental Aging Research* 25(4), 393–397.

15 A systematic literature review illustrated strong evidence for the benefits of offshoring in technology and indicated that it is a trend that is likely to continue Strasser, A.R.T.U.R. and Westner, M.A.R.K.U.S., 2015. Information systems offshoring: Results of a systematic literature review. *Journal of Information Technology Management* 26(2), 70–142.

16 Deloitte report https://www2.deloitte.com/content/dam/insights/us/articles/4674_IbtN-July-2018/DI_IbtN-July-2018.pdf (accessed 13.06.2019).

17 Rothwell, A., Herbert, I. and Seal, W., 2011. Shared service centres and professional employability. *Journal of Vocational Behavior* 79, 241–252.

18 Gratton, L., Scott, A. and Caulkin, S., 2016. 100 year life: A gift or a curse. *London Business School Review* 27(2), 40–43.

19 For more information, visit www.skillsfuture.sg/credit (accessed 24.04.2019).

20 Adkins, A. and Rigoni, B., 2016. Millennials want jobs to be development opportunities. *Gallop Business Journal.* https://www.gallup.com/workplace/236438/millennials-jobs-development-opportunities.aspx (accessed 20.08.2019).

21 For example, see Duffy, R. D., Autin, K. L. and Bott, E. M., 2015. Work volition and job satisfaction: Examining the role of work meaning and person – environment fit. *The Career Development Quarterly* 63(2), 126–140.

22 Schwab, 2017.

23 Shift happens first appeared in 2006. Planned as content for a staff development day by Karl Fisch, of Arapahoe High School in the USA, it has been published and modified by manner under a Creative Commons licence. It poses challenging questions about the future nature of work and the role of education.

24 EY report, 2016. The upside of disruption: Megatrends shaping 2016 and beyond, www.ey.com/gl/en/issues/business-environment/ey-megatrends (accessed 13.06.2019).

25 PwC 2018. Will robots really steal our jobs: An international analysis of the potential long term impact of automation, www.pwc.co.uk/economic-services/assets/international-impact-of-automation-feb-2018.pdf (accessed 13.06.2019).

26 The report was based on a 'rapid evidence review', conducted by our Loughborough colleagues Professor Hislop, D., Dr Coombs, C., Dr Taneva, S. and Dr Barnard, S., December 2017. *Impact of artificial intelligence, robotics and automation technologies on work.* CIPD.

27 For an example of how this works in practice, visit the customer stories via the Fuse website, https://fuse.fuseuniversal.com/communities/2086 (accessed 13.06.2019).

28 For example, see www.class-central.com/report/mooc-stats-2017/ (accessed 13.06.2019).

29 For examples of these see Arctic Shores, see www.arcticshores.com/; Hirevue www.hirevue.com/ (accessed 13.06.2019).

30 SHRM survey on 'Using Social Media for Talent Acquisition – recruitment and screening' 2015 www.shrm.org/hr-today/trends-and-forecasting/research-and-surveys/Documents/SHRM-Social-Media-Recruiting-Screening-2015.pdf (accessed 13.06.2019).

31 For example, see Arthur and Rousseau define career as '*the unfolding sequence of a person's work experiences over time*', Arthur, M. B. and Rousseau, D. M., 1996. *The boundaryless career.* Oxford: Oxford University Press.

32 For more information on thriving at work, see chapter seven.

33 For example, the idea of the 'boundaryless career' (Arthur and Rousseau, 1996). However, these changes have not yet had as much impact as predicted. For example, see Clarke, M., 2013. The organizational career: Not dead but in need of redefinition. *The International Journal of Human Resource Management* 24(4), 684–703.

34 For example, see Dries, N., 2011. The meaning of career success: Avoiding reification through a closer inspection of historical, cultural, and ideological contexts. *Career Development International* 16(4), 364–384.

35 For example, Clarke has described five propositions of a 'new organisational career', Clarke, 2013.

36 See the Mercr Global Talent Trends 2018 report. This can be downloaded from www.mmc.com/insights/publications/2018/jan/mercer-global-talent-trends-2018.html (accessed 26.04.2019).

37 To download the report, visit www.pwc.com/gx/en/people-organisation/pdf/pwc-preparing-for-tomorrows-workforce-today.pdf (accessed 26.04.2019).

38 Graeber, D., 2019. *Bullshit jobs: The rise of pointless work, and what we can do about it.* London: Penguin Books Ltd.

39 For example, see the research conducted within the EU by ACUMEN www.acumen.website/en/home/ (accessed 26.04.2019).

40 High social capital enables people to draw on the resources of others through strong networking and interpersonal skills. High social capital has been linked with high career success. For further information, see Adler, P. S. and Kwon, S. W., 2002. Social capital: Prospects for a new concept. *Academy of management review* 27(1), 17–40.

41 See endnote 38.

4

PROSOCIAL PRACTICES, POSITIVE IDENTITY, AND FLOURISHING AT WORK

Jane E. Dutton, Laura Morgan Roberts, and Jeff Bednar

When you think of yourself at work, how do you think you are faring? Are you flourishing at work, feeling a sense of engagement, motivation, growth, and learning, or is languishing a better descriptor for your state of well-being? This chapter explores one important way in which organizations shape our ability to flourish at work. As employees, we spend more time engaged with our work organizations than we do with our families, friends, or other institutions (Hochschild, 1997). New technologies are quickly blurring the boundaries between work and nonwork, amplifying work immersion for the average employee. In such a world, how do work organizations leave their imprint on employees, or, from a positive organizational psychology perspective, how do work contexts cultivate employee flourishing? In this chapter, we explore how work contexts cultivate employee flourishing through the way they shape the identities that employees construct at work.

We address this link between work contexts, identity, and employee flourishing through a focus on organizational practices. Organizational practices refer to the situated, recurrent activities that people engage in at work (Orlikowski, 2002). For example, organizations have distinct socialization practices to assist newcomers in joining the organization (Van Maanen & Schein, 1979). Research suggests that people come to define themselves positively as a result of socialization practices and are subsequently higher performers and are retained longer (Cable, Gino, & Staats, 2013). Organizational researchers have explored how organizational practices affect an organization's strategy (Jarzabkowski, 2004), the design of work (Barley, 1986), organizational learning (Antonacopoulou, 2006), and organizational performance (Cameron, Mora, & Leutscher, 2011). More recently, researchers have been exploring this potentially important link between organizational practices and the construction of employee identity (Bednar, Galvin, Ashforth, &

Hafermalz, in press; Carlsen, 2006; Michel, 2007), but there has been a dearth of research on how organizational practices shape work-related identities in ways that foster employee flourishing. A focus on what we call prosocial practices and positive work-related identities permits us to build this important conceptual link.

We build the core arguments of our chapter in four sequential steps. First, we introduce the idea of positive work-related identities (Dutton, Roberts, & Bednar, 2010; Roberts & Dutton, 2009). Next, we review research suggesting that positive work-related identities are linked to various indicators of flourishing. We note at the outset that few of these studies establish truly causal effects, so additional empirical research is required to validate these links. We then focus on a category of organizational practices—prosocial practices—that seem to have a potent effect on the way employees construct their identities at work. Finally, we outline a research agenda for positive organizational psychology to contribute to society through increasing our understanding of how organizational practices affect employees' identities and their ability to flourish at work.

Positive Work-Related Identities

Because work is a key domain in people's lives, involvement in work organizations is a critical source of identity (Ashforth & Mael, 1989; Dutton, Dukerich, & Harquail, 1994; Gini, 1998). The term "identity" refers to the way in which an individual constructs or defines him or herself (Gecas, 1982) and "work-related" identities are the meanings that individuals take on through their engagement with aspects of work, including professions, occupations, work-roles, or organizations (Dutton et al., 2010). As employees come to identify with certain aspects of their professions, occupations, work roles, or organizations, they often infuse their individual identities with the defining characteristics of these collectives or roles. For example, employees who joined Amway began to see themselves as free, family-oriented, altruistic, and successful as they engaged in various practices called "dream-building" (Pratt, 2000). Employees of the Port Authority (PA) of New York and New Jersey saw themselves as talented professionals who were building beautiful edifices and preserving New York City's symbols of global trade (Dutton & Dukerich, 1991). As a result, employees felt personally insulted when the PA was criticized by the media for inhumane treatment of homeless persons who were frequenting PA-run buildings (Dutton & Dukerich, 1991). These examples remind us that employees often take on qualities and characteristics of their work organizations and fuse them with their own self-constructions.

The desire to construct a positive identity is a central assumption in many psychological and sociological theories (Gecas, 1982; Turner, 1982). We build on this assumption by asking: What are the different ways in which an individual's work identity can be positive? A focus on positive work identities is a growing field of investigation in organizational studies (Roberts & Dutton, 2009; Roberts & Creary, 2012; Roberts, 2014). A review of research published in organizational psychology reveals that work-related identities can be positive in at least four different ways (Dutton et al., 2010): content (i.e., the attributes or characteristics that one uses to define him or herself include character strengths and virtues); subjective evaluation (i.e., the identity is regarded favorably); development (i.e., a person sees him or herself as growing in ways that promote maturity and adaptation); or structure (i.e., the multiple facets of one's identity are related in harmonious and complementary ways; Dutton et al., 2010). For example, a professor may find his or her professional identity to be positive because it is endowed with the virtue of wisdom; because it is evaluated positively by students; because it is on a trajectory of constant learning and progression; or because it facilitates compatibility and balance between multiple identities (i.e., researcher, teacher, consultant, parent). Each one of these theoretical perspectives on identity points to several different antecedents that cultivate positive identities and different outcomes that are associated with positive identities.

Positive Work-Related Identities and Flourishing

Dutton and colleagues argue that as employees' work-related identities become more positive, individuals are strengthened and become more capable of dealing with current challenges while identifying and taking advantage of new opportunities (Dutton et al., 2010). Here, we provide suggestive evidence that cultivating various forms of positive work-related identity also promotes employee flourishing more generally. These potential implications for flourishing help to justify why it is important to cultivate positive work-related identities. A variety of conceptual and empirical studies suggest that as employees' work-related identities become more positive, they experience enhanced psychological functioning, positive feelings, and social functioning (the three components of flourishing identified by Keyes's (1998) typology of mental health). For example, one indicator of healthy psychological functioning at work is work engagement. Work engagement is defined as a positive, fulfilling, personal state characterized by vigor (e.g., high levels of energy and mental resilience while working), dedication (e.g., significance, enthusiasm, inspiration, pride, and challenge), and absorption (e.g., being fully concentrated and happily engrossed in one's work; Hakanen, Perhoniemi, & Toppinen-Tanner, 2008). Research shows that positive self-evaluations of work-related identity are an important predictor of work engagement (Mauno, Kinnunen, & Ruokolainen, 2007; Xanthopoulou, Bakker, Demerouti, & Schaufeli, 2009). Moreover, cultivating an identity at work that is more virtue-based (e.g., understanding and utilizing one's strengths at work) is also related to work engagement (Harter, Schmidt, & Keyes, 2003). For example, one study found that as employees experienced more compassion at work, they viewed their work identities more positively and engaged in higher levels of organizational citizenship behaviors and exhibited lower levels of turnover (Moon, Hur, Ko, Kim & Yoo, 2016). Research also shows that work engagement is associated with

adaptive behaviors (e.g., personal initiative—see Hakanen et al., 2008) and ultimately affects "bottom-line" outcomes (e.g., profits, productivity, employee retention, and customer satisfaction; Harter et al., 2003). Taken together, this research
on work engagement suggests that cultivating a positive, work-related identity
helps individuals to flourish at work.

Other indicators of enhanced psychological functioning include self-acceptance,
personal growth, and environmental mastery, or the capacity to effectively manage one's life and surrounding world (Keyes, 1998; Ryff & Keyes, 1995). Research
on identity change during role challenges suggests that positive identities relate to
employee flourishing. For example, Ibarra's (2003) study of professionals in major
career transitions suggests that individuals who explore new possible selves at work
adapt more effectively to the demands of changing work environments and experience more coherence between who they are and what they do.

This research on psychological functioning further strengthens the claim that
cultivating positive identities at work helps individuals to flourish.

Positive identities also may link to flourishing through how they cultivate positive emotions. For example, Fine's (1996) work on restaurant cooks shows that
individuals draw on different rhetorics to shape how they think of themselves as
workers. These different self-views enable cooks to experience positive emotions
such as pride, enthusiasm, and honor, which promote occupational satisfaction,
creativity, and social cohesion (Fine, 1996). Positive emotions, in general, help
individuals to build cognitive and social resources, counteract the impact of negative emotions, and expand the terrain of possibilities for who an individual can
become (Fredrickson, 1998, 2009; see also Roberts, Dutton, Spreitzer, Heaphy, &
Quinn, 2005, for an organizational application).

A third way in which positive work-related identities promote flourishing is
by enhancing social well-being and promoting the adoption of behaviors that
build social coherence, social actualization, social integration, social acceptance, or
social contribution (Keyes, 1998). For example, a study by Dukerich, Golden, and
Shortell (2002) reports that physicians who evaluate their organization's identity
(i.e., the health system) more favorably are more willing to engage in cooperative
behaviors that will benefit other employees (e.g., extra-role behaviors) as well as
the healthcare system as a whole (e.g., referring patients to doctors within the
system). The work of Reed and Aquino (2003) suggests that as employees incorporate virtuous attributes and characteristics into their identity (what Reed and
Aquino call a moral identity), they will minimize ingroup/outgroup distinctions
and show increasing sympathy toward outgroup members. As these ingroup/
outgroup distinctions break down, social cohesion can increase in organizations
(Reed & Aquino, 2003). Further, constructing more positive work identities may
have a type of protective function (Karelaia & Guillen, 2014), insulating an individual from destructive identity conflicts that could hurt social interactions. These
studies on social functioning further substantiate the claim that cultivating more
positive identities at work can help employees to flourish.

The preliminary evidence that positive work-related identities may be psychologically and socially beneficial to employees raises the next logical question: How do different workplaces influence the way employees come to understand who they are? How can organizational practices shape or cultivate these forms of positive identity? The next section focuses on a particular kind of work practice that may be a powerful contributor to the construction of a positive identity at work.

Prosocial Practices and Positive Work-Related Identities

In organizational studies, there is a rich vein of research that examines organizational practices: the distinctive set of recurrent, patterned activities that characterize an organization (Orlikowski, 2002). These practices are part of an organization's signature, which shapes how the organization's knowledge is organized (Orlikowski, 2002), how resources are created (Feldman, 2004), how organizational learning occurs (Gherardi, 2006), and how organizational change occurs (Feldman & Pentland, 2003). While organizational researchers have focused on how specific human resource–related practices shape employee attitudes and actions (Losey, Meisinger, & Ulrich, 2005; Ulrich & Brockbank, 2005), they have devoted limited attention to how organizational practices impact employees' identities. Yet because organizational practices are linked to employee doing, and employee doing is linked to employee becoming (Bem, 1972; Carlsen, 2006), it seems logical and productive to ask: What organizational practices are conducive to the cultivation of positive work-related identities?

Our literature search revealed that a certain category of practices—prosocial practices—has a particularly potent influence on the way employees construct their identities. Prosocial practices are designed to protect and/or promote the welfare of other people and provide a conduit for employees to participate in routine helping and giving at work. Research in positive psychology indicates that engaging in helping others and giving to a cause that is larger than oneself promote flourishing (see Piliavin, 2003, for a review of the positive impacts of volunteering on the volunteer). While the direct effects of prosocial behavior outside of the workplace have been examined, such effects within the workplace have received far less attention. A ground-breaking line of research in this vein by Grant (Grant, 2007; Grant et al., 2007) and colleagues shows that engaging in prosocial practices at work often increases psychological and social functioning, as indicated by greater persistence, performance, and citizenship behaviors on the job (e.g., Grant, 2008a, 2008b; Grant et al., 2007; Grant & Mayer, 2009).

In this chapter, we expand this line of research by examining organizational practices that cultivate prosocial behavior and, more importantly, locate identity as a central mechanism that can explain why prosocial practices might promote flourishing at work. While a few studies show that engaging in helping behaviors increases self-evaluations (e.g., Newman, Vasudev, & Onawola, 1985), the central role of identity remains underexplored. We suggest that organizations that routinize employees' prosocial thoughts and behaviors through participation in institutionalized practices are more likely to cultivate employees' positive work-related identities. We detail findings from three field studies of employees' identification and/or commitment to their work organizations that provide evidential support for these core claims.

Employee Support Practices and Employees' Positive Identities

Many work organizations have provided opportunities for employees to participate in different types of employee support practices. Employee support practices include institutionalized procedures and routines that provide emotional, financial, and/or instrumental assistance to employees beyond pay, benefits, or recognition (Grant, Dutton, & Rosso, 2008). For some employee support practices, assistance to employees is provided directly by the organization, such as in child-care or elder-care programs (e.g., Cascio, 2003; Goodstein, 1995). Other practices provide opportunities for employee-to-employee helping or giving, such as when organizations allow employees to donate their vacation time to co-workers who need it (e.g., Griffin Hospital, as cited in Cameron, 2008, p. 11). Organizational researchers often examine how these practices shape employees' performance, commitment, or attachment to the organization (Perry-Smith & Blum, 2000; Trice & Beyer, 1984). For our purposes, we are interested in how these practices shape the kinds of identities that individuals construct at work.

Grant et al. (2008) conducted a survey and interview study of a Fortune 500 retail company (called Big Retail) to assess how employee participation in an employee support program (called the Employee Support Foundation, ESF) affected employee commitment. Participants in this program voluntarily granted permission for the company to deduct a dollar from their weekly paycheck. The company matched employee donations at a rate of 50 cents per dollar, and donations were pooled in a fund that employees could potentially draw from during crises such as illnesses, family deaths, or financial hardships. The ESF also provided educational scholarships and a bereavement response initiative. Therefore, this form of employee support program allowed employees to both receive and give support to their colleagues when faced with special needs. The 40 interviews and the employee survey revealed that there was a relationship between participation in the ESF and the employees' affective commitment and attachment to the organization. The results also suggested that participation in these programs changed the way individuals viewed the organization's identity and, by association, their own identity as an organizational member (Grant et al., 2008).

First, the interview study (20 store managers and 20 employees) consistently suggested that individuals took on a more positive identity by seeing themselves and the organization as more helpful, caring, and benevolent. While some researchers have called this a prosocial identity (Grant, 2007; Grant, Molinsky, Margolis, Kamin, & Schiano, 2009), this type of identity content implies that people are defining themselves with virtuous strengths or qualities such as kindness, generosity, care, compassion, niceness, and love (Peterson & Seligman, 2004). Several quotes illustrate the connection that employees felt between the ESF program, the company, and their identity. For example, managers discussed how participation in the program changed their capacity to help others:

> I have an employee . . . she was a young single mother . . . During the pregnancy, she switched from part-time to full-time, and in the process lost her insurance because she didn't read the packet completely . . . When we found out, I grabbed the ESF paperwork and started calling the ESF, and it was just the ability to help her through her pregnancy . . . It was good that there was somebody there that I could call and say, "Hey, this is what I've got, and can I help?" and to know that I was going to be able to help my employee . . . Because of the help that they've been to the employees . . . I feel good, because I know that there's somebody out there that it's helping.
>
> *(Manager #11; Grant et al., 2008, p. 903)*

The bolstered capacity to help and care for others allowed managers to see themselves as more caring individuals. This connection is clearly evident in this quote:

> I think it will always, I mean for the rest of my life, I will always be a more compassionate person. I always was, but more so now. Definitely nonjudgmental. You know like there's that saying "There but for the grace of God go I," you know, because I could be in their shoes tomorrow, and it doesn't really matter your education level, things happen to people, unexpected things. So they may not be prepared for them properly with insurance or whatever. So I think . . . I don't think a day will go by the rest of my life, that I won't think about the employees that were helped by the Foundation while I was involved.
>
> *(Manager, K8)*

While the interview study suggested that participation in the ESF increased employee commitment by changing how employees defined themselves and the company, the survey study provided an opportunity to test this association more rigorously (Grant et al., 2008). Using structural equation modeling to analyze survey responses from 240 employees, the authors found that the link between employee participation in the ESF and affective commitment to the company was partially mediated by the extent to which employees interpreted their identity and the organization's identity as caring and benevolent. Thus, in both qualitative and quantitative analyses there was evidence of a link between employees' participation in a prosocial practice and defining themselves and their organization in more positive, virtuous terms.

Community Outreach Practices and Employees' Positive Identities

Many organizations have also implemented community outreach practices for their employees. Community outreach practices refer to programs and routines that allow employees to provide assistance to groups outside of the employing organization in order to build ties between organizations and their communities (Bartel, 2001). Often these types of practices are implemented by organizations that have a strong social mission and wish to encourage employees to live out these mission claims through participation in the community (Besharov, 2014). These programs can be highly variable in terms of the kind of work (e.g., mentoring children, building structures, or delivering meals) and the length of time that they engage employees with outside groups (e.g., single-day encounters to year-long commitments). Depending on the organization, these programs may be called corporate citizenship programs, employee involvement programs, or corporate volunteer activities. As with the employee support programs, the practices enable and encourage employees in work organizations to engage in helping and contributing to others. However, for these programs, the recipients of help are individuals outside of the organization's boundaries.

Bartel (2001) was interested in whether employee participation in community outreach practices influenced employee levels of organizational identification, interpersonal cooperation, and effort. She designed a longitudinal field study to examine the impact of participation in outreach activities on employees at Pillsbury Company. The participants in her study completed pretest and posttest surveys along with self-report diaries at regular intervals. Supervisors also filled out surveys at the beginning and end of the employees' participation in the program.

Bartel's (2001) results suggest that employee participation in the program was associated with an increase in levels of identification, cooperation, and effort exerted on the job. When she analyzed what accounted for these changes, three mechanisms related to positive identity construction were apparent. First, interacting with members of other organizations while doing community work facilitated more intergroup comparisons. These intergroup comparisons left employees feeling better off and more fortunate than those with whom they compared themselves. Thus, this downward comparison process enhanced the participants' identities. Second, participation in these programs altered the employees' evaluations of their organization's identity. Participants began to see their organization as more cooperative, socially responsive, and innovative. Third, participation in the programs increased the employees' use of the organization's identity as a source of self-definition (as indicated by stronger levels of employer identification). As a result of these three different mechanisms, participants in community outreach programs developed more positive work-related identities.

Beneficiary Contact Practices

Finally, some work organizations grant employees exposure to the beneficiaries of their work. Grant and colleagues (Grant 2008a; Grant et al., 2007) have been exploring how this contact with the beneficiaries of work affects motivation and performance. This series of studies suggests that one reason beneficiary contact practices lead to increased persistence and motivation on the job is that they alter how employees define themselves. In particular, this work implies that practices facilitating awareness and learning about the positive impact that one's work has had on others helps employees to evaluate who they are more positively and can change the content of their identities. While none of these studies was designed to study positive identity mechanisms directly, the set of studies is suggestive that identity may partially account for how and why these practices have their effects.

One field experiment examined the impact of contact with the beneficiaries on call-center workers who were raising money for a university. In the experimental condition, the callers were provided with 10 minutes of contact with a scholarship recipient (the beneficiary), who explained to callers the difference the scholarship had made in his life. There were two control conditions—one with no beneficiary contact and one involving a letter from a beneficiary that described impact. Just 10 minutes of direct contact with the beneficiary resulted in significantly greater persistence (142% increase in phone time) and job performance (171% more money raised) one month later when compared with individuals in the two control conditions (Grant et al., 2007). In a second study designed to deepen understanding of why the interpersonal contact with beneficiaries was so important, Grant et al. (2007) used an experimental study to explore how interpersonal contact with beneficiaries affected an individual's self-perception (Grant et al., 2007, experiment 2). In this laboratory experiment, the subjects were exposed to the beneficiary of their work through a casual four-minute conversation before the experiment began. Again, the study showed the significant effect of beneficiary contact on task persistence. Importantly, the key mediator of this effect was perceived impact, which involved subjects seeing themselves as a helpful contributor to others. While perceived impact was not measured as an indicator of positive identity, discussions with subjects suggested that participants in the study who were exposed to the beneficiary saw themselves as more generous and helpful. Thus, these studies suggest that beneficiary contact makes prosocial characteristics (i.e., kind, benevolent, helpful, etc.) more accessible for self-definition.

In a related study designed to assess the effects of beneficiary impact on the employees' job dedication and helping, Grant (2008b) conducted a field experiment with lifeguards working at a community pool. In the beneficiary impact condition, Grant exposed lifeguards to stories of rescues performed by other lifeguards as a means of making salient the significance of their impact on others. One month later, supervisors' ratings of the lifeguards showed that lifeguards who received this task significance treatment were more dedicated to their jobs and more helpful to others. Debriefs with the lifeguards in the beneficiary impact condition suggested that these lifeguards had begun to see themselves more positively (what Grant, 2008b, called perceived social worth). Again, this study provides indirect evidence that exposure to the beneficiaries of one's work increases the positivity of an employee's work-related identity.

Discussion

This trio of studies provides suggestive evidence that organizational practices can shape how employees define themselves in ways that might pave the way for employee flourishing. The three studies we reviewed showed a pattern of how prosocial organizational practices cultivate more positive work-related identities. These prosocial practices—employee support, community outreach, and beneficiary impact practices—promote thoughts and actions that influence two aspects of identity: identity content and identity evaluation.

Identity content becomes more positive as individuals who participate in prosocial practices come to define themselves in more virtuous ways. Dutton et al. (2010) introduce the virtue perspective on positive identity to encompass certain qualities that are indicators of what some scholars have called the "master virtues" (Peterson & Seligman, 2004). Drawing from virtue ethics (e.g., Aristotle, 1984; MacIntyre, 1981), and discussed by philosophers and religious leaders across time, virtues are assumed to be morally good qualities that distinguish people of good character (Dahlsgaard, Peterson, & Seligman, 2005). When individuals use or claim these morally good qualities as self-defining features, then an identity becomes more positive. In the studies that we presented here, the individuals came to define themselves as more helpful, caring, generous, and benevolent as a result of engaging in prosocial organizational practices that benefit other employees and the external community.

As individuals engaged in prosocial organizational practices, the changes in identity content were often accompanied by changes in identity evaluations. Dutton et al. (2010) introduce the evaluative perspective to explain that identity evaluations are another important source of positivity in work-related identities. Identification with favorably regarded social groups such as organizations helps individuals to feel more positively about themselves, which is important for psychological and social functioning (Baumeister, 1999; Branscombe, Ellemers, Spears, & Doosje, 1999; Gecas, 1982; Hogg & Terry, 2001). As such, individuals strive to construct and maintain positively regarded identities at work (Ashforth & Kreiner, 1999; Elsbach & Kramer, 1996; Kreiner, Ashforth, & Sluss, 2006; Pierce & Gardner, 2004). Prosocial organizational practices facilitate behaviors that enhance the esteem in which employees hold their employing organization as a sponsor of such practices and themselves as members of the organization.

The links we have proposed in this chapter open up multiple opportunities for future research. First, research needs to consider and test *how* prosocial practices exert their effects on positive identities. The research we have reviewed suggests that multiple cognitive and behavioral pathways may be important. One pathway is the route of attribute salience. This account suggests that employee participation in certain organizational practices makes certain attributes (such as caring or generosity) more salient and accessible for self-definition (Markus & Kunda, 1986). A different cognitive path suggests that participation in certain prosocial practices makes social group memberships more salient and attractive for self-definition (e.g., I am a member of Big Retail). If the social group has desirable qualities (i.e., generous or caring), individuals will identify more strongly with the social group and incorporate these attributes into their own self-concepts. Prosocial practices can also cultivate positive identities via social comparisons, as we saw in the Bartel study. In this case, intergroup comparisons that are elicited during participation in the programs elevate regard for one's own group, thus creating a more positive work-related identity. Prosocial practices may reinforce ways of doing that create the foundations for ways of being (Carlsen, 2006). Thus, individuals who engage in behaviors that are more caring, generous, and giving actually become more caring, generous, and giving.

Prosocial practices may also engage a different form of motivation that Crocker and colleagues (Crocker, 2008; Crocker & Canevello, 2008) call an ecosystem perspective. These researchers provide evidence about the benefits of taking an ecocentric perspective toward life—placing greater importance on the needs and concerns of others than on the desires and drives of one's own ego. Prosocial practices provide a conduit through which employees can cultivate and exercise this type of ecocentric orientation at work by making compassionate instead of self-image goals more salient (Crocker & Canevello, 2008). When compassionate goals are operational, individuals behave differently towards each other (in terms of giving and providing support: Crocker & Canevello, 2008), which is likely to foster a more positive work identity in terms of defining oneself as being a more caring and generous person.

A final path through which prosocial practices may affect self-definition is suggested by Lyubomirsky (2007), who argues that kindness "can jumpstart a cascade of positive social consequences" (p. 130) by enabling people to take on the identity of someone who is compassionate and altruistic, and enhancing their experience of self-acceptance, self-esteem, and self-efficacy. These claims are supported by our analysis of the impact of organizational prosocial practices on positive work-related identities. Moreover, participating in programs that institutionalize prosocial behaviors (e.g., volunteering) has been shown to have several positive psychological and social benefits, and at times these benefits are more pronounced for those who are giving than for those receiving help (see Piliavin, 2003, for a review).

Future research should also consider a broader range of prosocial practices that may contribute to how employees construct themselves positively. Organizations have institutionalized various developmental practices that shape how employees see and define themselves at work. For example, mentoring practices create opportunities for more seasoned organizational members to facilitate the growth and development of new members (e.g., Ragins & Kram, 2007), thus allowing mentors to see themselves as contributors to others. Organizational evaluation and reward practices could also play a role in encouraging prosocial behavior and thereby affect the kinds of positive identities that employees construct. For example, some work organizations explicitly encourage and reward co-worker helping (e.g., Southwest Airlines fosters peer-to-peer contributing: Gittell, 2003). For example, do organizations that promote prosocial practices foster greater workplace courage (Koerner, 2014) or workplace compassion (Worline & Dutton, 2017) which then facilitates the construction of positive work identities? To date, empirical evidence suggests these possible links but more rigorous causal studies are needed to test these assertions. Future research might also consider which types of prosocial practices have the most potent and/or most enduring impact on employee self-constructions. Future research might also consider whether the mechanisms by which different types of practices shape employees' positive identities are similar or different.

Not all organizational practices designed to have prosocial impact are likely to motivate and engage employees to the same degree. Future research needs to systematically consider factors that limit the capacity of prosocial practices to cultivate positive identities. For example, Grant (2008a) has shown that when employees have choice and discretion over participating in prosocial actions, they have higher levels of sustained motivation to act than when such choice or discretion is limited. In addition, some practices may have less impact on employees' self-construals because beneficiaries are more distant, which can undermine the meaning and pride that a person derives from beneficiary contact in prosocial actions. Keyes and Haidt (2003) also suggest that intense—rather than sporadic—involvement in prosocial behavior (i.e., several times a day rather than one day a month) is likely to have a greater impact on those who engage in such behavior.

Finally, future research needs to consider how other features of work organizations are likely to amplify or depress the impact of prosocial practices on positive work-related identities. For example, we know that an organization's leadership plays a significant role in shaping the meaning that individuals make of the work organizations they are a part of (Podolny, Khurana, & Hill-Popper, 2005). A leader's actions can reinforce the significance of acting in a prosocial way, and his or her actions can model appropriate actions that make it easier for employees to act prosocially. In organizations in which leaders' actions are consistent with the purposes and values implied by the prosocial practices, there should be stronger links to the positive identities of employees. For example, an in-depth study of how one organization responded compassionately to harm incurred by its members provided evidence of this link (Dutton, Worline, Frost, & Lilius, 2006). A leader's symbolic actions made at a critical time amplified organizational members' awareness of acting in a caring way, speeding up and magnifying the prosocial (compassionate) response of individuals.

Conclusions

This chapter has begun to till the fertile ground in applied organizational psychology that asks: How do work organizations make a difference for employee flourishing? It has begun to address this question by considering how institutionalized programs and practices shape how employees define themselves. When organizational practices institutionalize ways of doing and being that involve helping, giving, and contributing to others (inside or outside the organization), then work organizations create the content and context for individuals to take on more positive work-related identities. Our hope is that work organizations can participate in improving society through a more mindful consideration of how the practices they deploy shape the identities that employees construct and how these positive identities can be vital personal resources that contribute to flourishing at work and beyond.

In sum, our focus on the impacts of prosocial practices illuminates relationships between the three pillars of positive psychology: positive subjective experiences of the past, present, and future; positive individuals (i.e., a strengths-based conception of human nature); and positive institutions (Seligman, 2002; Seligman & Csikszentmihalyi, 2000). The third pillar—positive institutions—has received relatively less attention in the field of positive psychology compared to the study of positive emotion and individual strengths. This chapter develops work on positive institutions and illuminates one way in which positive institutions (prosocial practices) help to create more positive individuals (by facilitating positive identity construction), leading to more positive subjective experiences (employees flourish at work).

Acknowledgment

Thanks to Adam Grant for comments on an earlier version of this chapter.

References

Antonacopoulou, E. P. (2006). The relationship between individual and organizational learning: New evidence from managerial learning practices. *Management Learning, 37*, 454–473.

Aristotle. (1984). *The complete works of Aristotle*. Princeton, NJ: Princeton University Press.

Ashforth, B., & Kreiner, G. (1999). How can you do it? Dirty work and the challenge of constructing a positive identity. *Academy of Management Review, 24*, 413–434.

Ashforth, B., & Mael, F. (1989). Social identity theory and the organization. *Academy of Management Review, 14*, 20–39.

Barley, S. R. (1986). Technology as an occasion for structuring: Evidence from observations of CT scanners and the social order of radiology departments. *Administrative Science Quarterly, 31*, 78–108.

Bartel, C. A. (2001). Social comparisons in boundary-spanning work: Effects of community outreach on members' organizational identity and identification. *Administrative Science Quarterly, 46*, 379–414.

Baumeister, R. F. (1999). The self. In D. T. Gilbert, S. T. Fiske, & G. Lindzey (Eds.), *The handbook of social psychology* (4th ed., pp. 680–740). Boston: McGraw-Hill.

Bednar, J. S., Galvin, B. M., Ashforth, B. E., & Hafermalz, E. (in press). Putting identification in motion: A dynamic view of organizational identification. *Organization Science*.

Bem, D. J. (1972). Self perception theory. In L. Berkowitz (Ed.), *Advances in experimental social psychology* (Vol. 6, pp. 1–62). New York: Academic Press.

Besharov, M. L. (2014). The relational ecology of identification: How organizational identification emerges when individuals hold divergent values, *Academy of Management Journal, 57*, 1485–1512.

Branscombe, N. R., Ellemers, N., Spears, R., & Doosje, B. (1999). The context and content of social identity threat. In N. Ellemers & R. Spears (Eds.), *Social identity: Context, commitment, content* (pp. 35–58). Oxford: Blackwell.

Cable, D. M., Gino, F., & Staats, B. (2013). Breaking them in or eliciting their best? Reframing socialization around newcomers' authentic self-expression. *Administrative Science Quarterly, 58*, 1–36.

Cameron, K. (2008). *Positive leadership: Strategies for extraordinary performance*. San Francisco, CA: Berrett-Koehler.

Cameron, K., Mora, C., & Leutscher, T. (2011). Effects of positive practices on organizational effectiveness. *The Journal of Applied Behavioral Science, 47*, 266–308.

Carlsen, A. (2006). Organizational becoming as dialogic imagination of practice: The case of the indomitable Gauls. *Organization Science, 17*, 132–149.

Cascio, W. F. (2003). Changes in workers, work, and organizations. In W. Borman, R. Klimoski, & D. Ilgen (Eds.), *Handbook of psychology: Industrial and organizational psychology* (Vol. 12, pp. 401–422). New York: John Wiley & Sons.

Crocker, J. (2008). *From egosystem to ecosystem: Implications for learning, relationships, and well-being.* Washington, DC: American Psychological Association.

Crocker, J., & Canevello, A. (2008). Creating and undermining social support in communal relationships: The role of compassionate self-image goals. *Journal of Personality and Social Psychology, 95*, 555–575.

Dahlsgaard, K., Peterson, C., & Seligman, M. (2005). Shared virtue: The convergence of valued human strengths across culture and history. *Review of General Psychology, 9*, 202–213.

Dukerich, J. M., Golden, B. R., & Shortell, S. M. (2002). Beauty is in the eye of the beholder: The impact of organizational identification, identity, and image on the cooperative behaviors of physicians. *Administrative Science Quarterly, 47*, 507–533.

Dutton, J. E., & Dukerich, J. M. (1991). Keeping an eye on the mirror: Image and identity in organizational adaptation. *Academy of Management Journal, 34*, 517–554.

Dutton, J. E., Dukerich, J. M., & Harquail, C. V. (1994). Organizational images and member identification. *Administrative Science Quarterly, 39*, 239–263.

Dutton, J. E., Roberts, L. M., & Bednar, J. S. (2010). Pathways for positive identity construction at work: Four types of positive identity and the building of social resources. *Academy of Management Review, 35*, 265–293.

Dutton, J. E., Worline, M. C., Frost, P. J., & Lilius, J. (2006). Explaining compassion organizing. *Administrative Science Quarterly, 51*, 59–96.

Elsbach, K., & Kramer, R. (1996). Members' responses to organizational identity threats: Encountering and countering the business week rankings. *Administrative Science Quarterly, 41*, 442–476.

Feldman, M. S. (2004). Resources in emerging structures and processes of change. *Organization Science, 15*, 295–309.

Feldman, M. S., & Pentland, B. T. (2003). Reconceptualizing organizational routines as a source of flexibility and change. *Administrative Science Quarterly, 48*, 94–118.

Fine, G. A. (1996). Justifying work: Occupational rhetorics as resources in restaurant kitchens. *Administrative Science Quarterly, 41*, 90–115.

Fredrickson, B. L. (1998). What good are positive emotions. *Review of General Psychology, 2*, 300–319.

Fredrickson, B. L. (2009). *Positivity*. New York: Crown.

Gecas, V. (1982). The self-concept. *Annual Review of Sociology, 8*, 1–33.

Gherardi, S. (2006). *Organizational knowledge: The texture of organizing*. Oxford: Blackwell.

Gini, A. (1998). Work, identity and self: How we are formed by the work we do. *Journal of Business Ethics, 17*, 707–714.

Gittell, J. H. (2003). *The Southwest airlines way: Using the power of relationships to achieve high performance*. New York: McGraw-Hill.

Goodstein, J. (1995). Employer involvement in eldercare: An organizational adaptation perspective. *Academy of Management Journal, 38*, 1657–1671.

Grant, A. M. (2007). Relational job design and the motivation to make a prosocial difference. *Academy of Management Review, 32*, 393–417.

Grant, A. M. (2008a). Does intrinsic motivation fuel the prosocial fire? Motivational synergy in predicting persistence, performance, and productivity. *Journal of Applied Psychology, 93*, 48–58.

Grant, A. M. (2008b). The significance of task significance: Job performance effects, relational mechanisms, and boundary conditions. *Journal of Applied Psychology, 93*, 108–124.

Grant, A. M., Campbell, E. M., Chen, G., Cottone, K., Lapedis, D., & Lee, K. (2007). Impact and the art of motivation maintenance: The effects of contact with beneficiaries on persistence behavior. *Organizational Behavior and Human Decision Processes, 103*, 53–67.

Grant, A. M., Dutton, J. E., & Rosso, B. D. (2008). Giving commitment: Employee support programs and the prosocial sensemaking process. *Academy of Management Journal, 51*, 898–918.

Grant, A. M., & Mayer, D. M. (2009). Good soldiers and good actors: Prosocial and impression management motives as interactive predictors of affiliative citizenship behavior. *Journal of Applied Psychology, 94*, 900–912.

Grant, A. M., Molinsky, A., Margolis, J., Kamin, M., & Schiano, W. (2009). The performer's reactions to procedural injustice: When prosocial identity reduces prosocial behavior. *Journal of Applied Social Psychology, 39*, 319–349.

Hakanen, J. J., Perhoniemi, R., & Toppinen-Tanner, S. (2008). Positive gain spirals at work: From job resources to work engagement, personal initiative and work-unit innovativeness. *Journal of Vocational Behavior, 73*, 78–91.

Harter, J., Schmidt, F., & Keyes, C. (2003). Well-being in the workplace and its relationship to business outcomes: A review of the Gallup Studies. In C. Keyes & J. Haidt (Eds.), *Flourishing: Positive psychology and the life well lived* (pp. 205–224). Washington, DC: American Psychological Association.

Hochschild, A. (1997). *The time bind*. New York: Henry Holt & Co.

Hogg, M. A., & Terry, D. J. (2001). Social identity theory and organizational processes. In M. A. Hogg & D. J. Terry (Eds.), *Social identity processes in organizational contexts* (pp. 1–12). Philadelphia: Psychology Press.

Ibarra, H. (2003). *Working identity: Unconventional strategies for reinventing.* Cambridge, MA: Harvard Business School Press.

Jarzabkowski, P. (2004). Strategy as practice: Recursiveness, adaptation, and practices-in-use. *Organization Studies, 25,* 529–560.

Karelaia, N., & Guillen, L. (2014). Me, a woman and a leader: Positive social identity and identity conflict. *Organizational Behavior and Human Decision Processes, 125,* 204–219.

Keyes, C. (1998). Social well-being. *Social Psychology Quarterly, 61,* 121–140.

Keyes, C., & Haidt, J. (2003). *Flourishing: Positive psychology and the life well lived.* Washington, DC: American Psychological Association.

Koerner, M. (2014). Courage as identity work: Accounts of workplace courage. *Academy of Management Journal, 57,* 63–93.

Kreiner, G., Ashforth, B., & Sluss, D. (2006). Identity dynamics in occupational dirty work: Integrating social identity and system justification perspectives. *Organization Science, 17,* 619–636.

Losey, M., Meisinger, S., & Ulrich, D. (2005). *The future of human resource management.* Hoboken, NJ: John Wiley & Sons.

Lyubomirsky, S. (2007). *The how of happiness: A scientific approach to getting the life you want.* New York: Penguin Press.

MacIntyre, A. (1981). *After virtue.* South Bend, IN: Notre Dame Press.

Markus, H., & Kunda, Z. (1986). Stability and malleability of the self-concept. *Journal of Personality and Social Psychology, 51,* 858–866.

Mauno, S., Kinnunen, U., & Ruokolainen, M. (2007). Job demands and resources as antecedents of work engagement: A longitudinal study. *Journal of Vocational Behavior, 70,* 149–171.

Michel, A. A. (2007). A distributed cognition perspective on newcomers' change processes: The management of cognitive uncertainty in two investment banks. *Administrative Science Quarterly, 52,* 507–557.

Moon, T, Hur, W., Ko, S., Kim, J., & Yoo, D. (2016). Positive work-related identity as a mediator of the relationship between compassion at work and employee outcomes. *Human Factors and Ergonomics in Manufacturing and Service Industries, 26,* 84–94.

Newman, S., Vasudev, J., & Onawola, R. (1985). Older volunteers' perceptions of impacts of volunteering on their psychological well-being. *Journal of Applied Gerontology, 4,* 123–134.

Orlikowski, W. (2002). Knowing in practice: Enacting a collective capability in distributed organizing. *Organization Science, 13,* 249–273.

Perry-Smith, J. E., & Blum, T. C. (2000). Work—family human resource bundles and perceived organizational performance. *Academy of Management Journal, 43,* 1107–1117.

Peterson, C., & Seligman, M. (2004). *Character strengths and virtues: A handbook and classification.* Washington, DC: American Psychological Association.

Pierce, J. L., & Gardner, D. G. (2004). Self-esteem within the work and organizational context: A review of the organization-based self-esteem literature. *Journal of Management, 30,* 591–622.

Piliavin, J. (2003). Doing well by doing good: Benefits for the benefactor. In C. Keyes & J. Haidt (Eds.), *Flourishing: Positive psychology and the life well lived* (pp. 227–247). Washington, DC: American Psychological Association.

Podolny, J., Khurana, R., & Hill-Popper, M. (2005). Revisiting the meaning of leadership. *Research Organizational Behavior, 26*, 1–36.

Pratt, M. G. (2000). The good, the bad, and the ambivalent: Managing identification among Amway distributors. *Administrative Science Quarterly, 45*, 456–493.

Ragins, B., & Kram, K. (2007). *The handbook of mentoring at work: Theory, research and practice.* Thousand Oaks, CA: Sage Publications.

Reed II, A., & Aquino, K. F. (2003). Moral identity and the expanding circle of moral regard toward out-groups. *Journal of Personality and Social Psychology, 84*, 1270–1286.

Roberts, L. (2014). Cultivate positive identities. In J. Dutton & G. Spreitzer (Eds.), *How to be a positive leader* (pp. 55–64.) San Francisco, CA: Berrett-Koehler Publisher.

Roberts, L., & Creary, S. (2012). Positive identity construction: Insights from classical and contemporary approaches. In K. Cameron & G. Spreitzer (Eds.), *Handbook of positive organizational scholarship* (pp. 70–83). New York: Oxford University Press.

Roberts, L. M., & Dutton, J. E. (2009). *Exploring positive identities and organizations: Building a theoretical and research foundation.* New York: Psychology Press.

Roberts, L. M., Dutton, J. E., Spreitzer, G. M., Heaphy, E. D., & Quinn, R. E. (2005). Composing the reflected best self-portrait: Building pathways for becoming extra-ordinary in work organizations. *Academy of Management Review, 30*, 712–736.

Ryff, C. D., & Keyes, C. L. M. (1995). The structure of psychological well-being revisited. *Journal of Personality and Social Psychology, 69*, 719–727.

Seligman, M. (2002). *Authentic happiness: Using the new positive psychology to realize your potential for lasting fulfillment.* New York: Free Press.

Seligman, M., & Csikszentmihalyi, M. (2000). Positive psychology: An introduction. *American Psychologist, 55*, 5–14.

Trice, H. M., & Beyer, J. M. (1984). Employee assistance programs: Blending performance-oriented and humanitarian ideologies to assist emotionally disturbed employees. *Research in Community and Mental Health, 4*, 245–297.

Turner, J. C. (1982). Toward a cognitive redefinition of the social group. In H. Tajfel (Ed.), *Social identity and intergroup relations* (pp. 15–40). Cambridge: Cambridge University Press.

Ulrich, D., & Brockbank, W. (2005). *The HR value proposition.* Cambridge, MA: Harvard Business School Press.

Van Maanen, J., & Schein, E. H. (1979). Towards a theory of organizational socialization. In B. M. Staw (Ed.), *Research in organizational behavior* (pp. 209–264). Greenwich, CT: JAI Press.

Worline, M., & Dutton, J. (2017). *Awakening compassion at work.* San Jose: Berrett-Koehler Publishers.

Xanthopoulou, D., Bakker, A. B., Demerouti, E., & Schaufeli, W. B. (2009). Work engagement and financial returns: A diary study on the role of job and personal resources. *Journal of Occupational and Organizational Psychology, 82*, 183–200.

5

UNDERSTANDING THE ROLE OF PERSONAL COPING STRATEGY IN DECREASING WORK AND FAMILY CONFLICT

A Cross-Cultural Perspective

Anit Somech and Anat Drach-Zahavy

In recent decades, social trends have stimulated a burgeoning interest in work-family conflict (WFC) and its antecedents and consequences (Korabik, Whitehead, & Lero, 2008). However, little research has focused on personal coping strategy for better understanding the WFC phenomenon by specifying the unique styles that individuals use to deal with WFC or identifying among these styles the ones most effective in lowering the conflict level. Moreover, to date, no previous global study has examined cross-national differences in individual coping strategies to ease WFC. Studying coping strategy from a cross-cultural perspective is crucial for several reasons. First, scholars (e.g., Kuo, 2011; Lazarus & Folkman, 1984) have argued theoretically that a person's internalized cultural values, beliefs, and norms affect the appraisal process of stressors, hence the perceived appropriateness of coping responses, although this has not been empirically demonstrated. Second, although coping is a universal experience faced by individuals regardless of culture, ethnicity, and race, members of different cultures might consider and respond to stressors differently with respect to coping goals, strategies, and outcomes (Chun, Moos, & Cronkite, 2006; Lam & Zane, 2004). Further, understanding cultural differences regarding how individuals cope with WFC is necessary for global organizations, but also for domestic organizations with a multicultural workforce. To effectively manage diversity, these organizations seek to develop employees' skills to balance work and family that are sensitive to cultural differences. Studying the influence of culture on WFC and coping will also help managers in non-Western contexts (e.g., emerging economies) who need to understand the applicability of coping strategies that are developed in Western industrialized societies (Gelfand & Knight, 2005).

In this chapter, we sought to help fill a critical void in WFC research by exploring cross-national differences in individual coping strategies to ease such conflict. We developed a classification of countries on two key dimensions that are critical for WFC research: "individualism-collectivism" and "gender-role ideology." Individualism-collectivism (I-C), though well researched in cross-cultural and cross-national studies, and an important variable in the work-family domain (e.g., Spector et al., 2004; Yang, Chen, Choi, & Zou, 2000), as a classification that relies on a single dimension might lead to over-generalization. To capture the complexity of the WFC phenomenon, research needs to move beyond simple dichotomies of individualism-collectivism (Gelfand & Knight, 2005). Specifically, this chapter discusses the role of culture in shaping the strategies employees use to cope with WFC, as well as their effectiveness.

Conceptual Background and Hypotheses

Personal Coping with W-F Conflict—A Cross-Cultural Perspective

Given the extensive study of coping in the stress literature (cf. Folkman & Moskowitz, 2004), it is puzzling to find a relative lack of research on coping in the context of work and family (e.g., Behson, 2002; Somech & Drach-Zahavy, 2007). Coping with WFC is defined here as the cognitive and behavioral efforts individuals make to manage the stresses arising from the conflicting demands of the work and family domains. According to the Conservation of Resources Theory (Hobfoll, 1989, 2001), when stress levels rise, individuals expend internal or external resources to manage the distress. The resources that the person possesses are internal; they encompass personal characteristics such as efficacy, optimism, and coping styles; external resources do not belong to the person but are available from his/her external environment. In the context of this chapter, using personal coping with WFC in an effort to manage conflicting work and family demands might be seen as reliance on internal resources. In this vein, Somech and Drach-Zahavy (2007) developed and refined an eight-strategy typology. The strategies denoted behavioral aspects of coping that specify what individuals actually do at work and/or at home to cope with WFC: *Good enough at home/work*—lowering the performance of family/work responsibilities to a less than perfect level; *Super at home/work*—insisting on doing all family/work duties single-handedly and perfectly; *Delegation at home/work*—managing one's own family/work duties by delegating some to others; and *Priorities at home/work*—arranging family/work duties in order of priority, and undertaking only those with high priority.

WFC is bidirectional, consisting of two components: work interference with family (WIF) and family interference with work (FIW). Given the multiple ways individuals cope with WIF and FIW, we suggest that no coping styles are universally appropriate; some may work better with specific forms of conflict within specific contexts. In particular, we suggest that countries' cluster (operationalized to represent the combination of I-C and gender-role ideology) may moderate the relationship of personal coping and WIF and FIW. WFC and its related issues are inherently a cultural phenomenon (Gelfand & Knight, 2005). Culture has both constitutive and regulatory effects that shape how people act in the domains of work and family. The constitutive effects of culture refer to the way in which the value and significance that individuals attach to different objects and behaviors are shaped by their cultural environment. Thus, what individuals perceive as desirable in terms, for example, of their investment in work and/or family will be influenced by their cultural values and norms. The regulatory effects of culture refer to the way in which social norms, customs, and conventions define the legitimate sets of roles and activities for different individuals in each society (Thein, Austen, Currie, & Lewin, 2010). Work and family pressures reflect social expectations and self-expectations and are most susceptible to values and beliefs internalized through socialization (Parasuraman, Purohit, Godshalk, & Beutell, 1996; Yang et al., 2000). Similarly, divisions of work and family roles tend to differ according to cultural values (Trompenaars & Hampton-Turner, 1998).

Systematic cross-cultural comparisons of WFC are few, and those that exist focus mostly on the antecedents and consequences of WFC (Lu et al., 2009). Many of these studies have adopted individualism-collectivism (I-C) as a general explanatory framework for cultural differences, and found that nation (operationalized to represent I-C) moderated the relation of work/family demands to WFC (e.g., Lu, Gilmour, Kao, & Huang, 2006; Spector et al., 2004; Yang et al., 2000). Although I-C is a construct well researched in cross-cultural and cross-national studies, research apparently needs to move beyond simple dichotomies of individualism—collectivism to capture the complexity of the WFC phenomenon (Gelfand & Knight, 2005). In one of the rare studies that refer to the combination of I-C and power distance, Lu et al. (2009) examined the relation of work resources (supervisory support and organizational family supportive values), WFC, and work- and nonwork-related outcomes, comparing samples of Taiwanese and British employees. They found that supervisory support had a stronger protective effect for Taiwanese than British employees. However, to date, no study has examined the role of individual coping strategy in decreasing WIF and FIW taking a cross-cultural perspective.

Individualism-collectivism is an analytical dimension that captures the relative importance people accord to personal interests and to shared pursuits (Wagner, 1995). Individualistic cultures emphasize self-reliance, autonomy, control, and priority of personal goals, which may or may not be consistent with in-group goals. An individual feels proud of his or her own accomplishments and derives satisfaction from performance based on his or her own achievements. By contrast, in collectivistic cultures people will subordinate their personal interests to the goals of their in-group. An individual belongs to only a few in-groups, and behavior within the group emphasizes goal attainment, cooperation, and group welfare and harmony. Thus, pleasure and satisfaction derive from group accomplishment (Lam, Chen, & Schaubroeck, 2002; Triandis, 1995). In a cultural norm of individualism, people tend to keep work and family relationships separate, while collectivists usually integrate the two realms. The collectivist culture legitimizes giving priority to work, and investing extra effort in work is considered self-sacrifice for the benefit of the family rather than sacrifice of the family for the selfish pursuit of one's own career as in an individualistic culture (Lu et al., 2006).

Gender-role ideology is conceived as beliefs and opinions about the ways that family and work roles do and should differ based on sex (Harris & Firestone, 1998), and these typically lie on a continuum from traditional to egalitarian. Traditional attitudes to gender roles reinforce or conform to expected differences in roles for men and women, while egalitarian attitudes do not believe in role segregation according to gender, and hold more equal views of the roles of women and men at home as well as work. Gender-role attitude, like any other, is learned through experience (Lachman, 1991). Strong forces of socialization and gender-role norms teach children at very young ages that certain roles or jobs are identified with men or with women (Firestone, Harris, & Lambert, 1999). For example, the research of Marini, Fan, Finely, and Beutel (1996) on the influence of job values (i.e., what people want in a job) on youth indicated that these values had a stronger influence on job choice than other background variables.

To classify the 10 countries according to the two dimensions of I-C and gender-role ideology, we conducted a cluster analysis, which is described in Chapter 2. The results revealed three subgroups: (1) high in individualism and a more egalitarian gender-role ideology (I-E group), which includes Australia, Canada, Spain, and the United States; (2) high in collectivism, and a more traditional gender-role ideology (C-T group), which includes China, India, Indonesia, and Turkey; and (3) average ratings in both dimensions (MC-MT), which includes Israel and Taiwan.

Thinking about the implications of these differences suggests that variations in I-C combined with variation in gender-role ideology might serve as a moderator in the relation of coping strategy to WFC. With respect to WFC coping strategies, we expected effective coping to reduce the level of WFC. If an employed parent is coping effectively, his/her perceived WFC should be lower because the conflict is "under control," so to speak. Similarly, perceived conflict should be highest in those who ineffectively or inefficiently manage WFC (Lazarus, 1991; Rotondo, Carlson, & Kincaid, 2003). Given the multiple ways individuals cope with stress, we suggest that no coping styles are universally appropriate; some may work better in specific contexts. In particular, because the combination of I-C and gender-role ideology (represented by group) is expected to affect the extent in which work and family are perceived as distinct domains, and their relative priority, we expected that the effectiveness of specific coping styles in attenuating WIF and FIW would vary depend on cultural differences (Somech & Drach-Zahavy, 2007).

Specifically, the I-E group consisted of people with high individualism together with an egalitarian gender-role ideology. Their self-definition, which is the pursuit of personal gains, emphasizes personal accomplishment and achievement through work (Spector et al., 2004); but they also have a more even attitude to the role of women and men at home as well as at work. Previous studies (Lu et al., 2010) showed that although people in this group value personal achievement through work more than fulfillment of family obligations, they often perceive sacrificing family resources for work as failure to meet their role as parent or spouse. For these individuals (men and women) any coping strategy that allows them personal accomplishment through work (i.e., super at work), but also to function as parents and spouses (i.e., priorities at work/home, delegation at work/home), might serve as an effective technique to lessen WFC. Any technique that distances them from their role at work (i.e., super at home, good enough at work) or at home (i.e., good enough at home) should raise the level of WIF and FIW.

> *Hypothesis 1: For the I-E group, for men and women alike, the coping strategies of super at work will decrease the level of FIW; while priorities at work/home and delegation at work/home will decrease the level of WIF.*

The C-T group consists of people with high collectivism and a traditional gender-role ideology. These employed parents place group interests above individual preferences. Investing extra effort in work is considered as self-sacrifice for the benefit of the family rather than sacrifice of the family for the selfish pursuit of their own career, as it is in an individualistic culture (Lu et al., 2006). However, their more traditional gender-role ideology means that men should invest extra efforts in work for the benefit of the family, while women should sustain their primary role as wives and mothers and invest less effort in work. A coping strategy that allows men to maintain high standards at work (i.e., super at work and good enough at home), and one that allows women to maintain high standards at home (i.e., super at home, and good enough at work), might serve as an effective technique to lessen WIF and FIW. Coping techniques that run counter to their values and beliefs will cause greater WIF and FIW.

> *Hypothesis 2a: For men in the C-T group, the coping strategies of super at work and good enough at home will decrease FIW and WIF.*

> *Hypothesis 2b: For women in the C-T group, the coping strategies of super at home and good enough at work will decrease FIW and WIF.*

People in the third group (MC-MT) evince medium levels of collectivism and of the traditional gender-role ideology, although to some extent, women are expected to be responsible for the home and men for the family's material well-being; men don't want their paid work to distract them from their family, and women don't want their home obligations to distract them from their paid work (Hassan, Dollard, & Winefield, 2010). We expect that any coping strategy that allows these men and women to balance work and family (i.e., priorities at home/work, delegation at home/work) might ease WIF and FIW, while any technique that distances them for one of these roles (i.e., super at home and good enough at work for men, and super at work and good enough at home for women) will raise the level of WIF and FIW.

> *Hypothesis 3: For men and women in the MC-MT the coping strategies of priorities at home/work, delegation at home/work will decrease the levels of WIF and FIW.*

Findings

Figure 15.1 depicts the distribution of coping strategies usage by group, showing that for the I-E group the most common coping strategy was *delegation at home* (M = 3.88), followed by *good enough at home* (M = 3.87), and then *super at work* (M = 3.40); the three least frequently used coping strategies were *priorities at home* (M = 2.78), *super at home* (M = 2.87), and *good enough at work* (M = 2.87). For the MC-MT group, the most common coping strategy was *delegation at home* (M = 4.04), followed by *delegation at work* (M = 3.62), and *super at work* (M = 3.61); the least frequently used coping strategies were *priorities at home* (M = 2.78) and *good enough at work* (M = 2.87). For the C-T group the most common coping strategy was *delegation at home* (M = 3.71), followed by *super at work* (M = 3.62); the least frequently used coping strategies were *priorities at home* (M = 2.78) and *good enough at home* (M = 3.41). Although the results indicated some consistency in the pattern of coping-strategy usage, the findings pointed to significant differences among the three groups in the means. For example, for *delegation at home* the MC-MT group reported the highest mean, followed by the mean of the I-E group, while the C-T group reported it as the least frequently used. Only for *super at work* was there was no difference in means among the three groups.

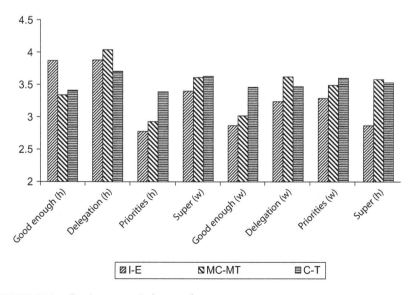

FIGURE 15.1   Coping strategies' means by group.

Testing the Proposed Model

To test our main hypothesis that the interactive effect of culture (group) and gender moderates the relationship between coping strategy and WIF and FIW, we conducted a series of hierarchical regressions to predict WIF and FIW. First, we compared the I-E group with the other two groups, coding I-E as 0 and MC-MT or C-T as 1. Next, we compared I-E (0) with MC-MT (1), and I-E (0) with C-T (1).

In each analysis the control variables (number of children living at home, job schedule, job position) were entered in step 1. The main effect terms of the proposed predictors, namely group, gender, and the eight coping strategies were entered in step 2, the second-order interactive effect of group and coping strategy term in step 3, and the third-order interactive effect of group, gender and coping strategy term in step 4. The models are summarized in Table 15.1 and Figures 15.2 and 15.3.

First, regarding the comparison of I-E group with the other two groups, the results for the prediction of WIF indicated that the control variables accounted for .03% of the variance in this conflict, and the joint main effects of WIF predictors accounted for an additional 24%. The second-order interaction effects between group and coping strategy entered in step 3 accounted for an additional 6.97%, and the third-order interaction effects between group, gender, and coping strategy

TABLE 15.1 Results of hierarchical regression analyses for predicting WIF and FIW.

Step Variables	I-E vs. Others		I-E vs. MC-MT		I-E vs. C-T	
	WIF	FIW	WIF	FIW	WIF	FIW
	b	b	b	b	b	b
Step 1: Control Variables						
ΔF	31.34**	6.18**	4.15*	3.92*	31.34**	6.18**
DF	3	3	3	3	3	3
Constant	3.15**	2.69**	3.58**	2.75**	3.15**	2.69**
Number of children	.02	-.05*	.01	.01	.02	-.05*
Schedule of job	.41**	.15**	.23**	-.17*	.41**	.15**
Job position	.15**	-.03	.01	-.07	.15**	-.03
Step 2: Main Effects						
ΔF	94.81**	65.02**	48.91**	28.31**	94.81**	60.12**
DF	13	13	13	13	13	13
Super (H)	-.01	.02	.04	.10**	-.01	.03*
Good enough (H)	.33**	.15**	.38**	.12**	.32**	.15**
Delegation (H)	.05**	.03	.02	.02	.04*	.03
Priorities (H)	.02	.02	-.01	.03	.02	.03
Super (W)	-.01	-.06**	.03	.01	-.01	-.06**

Step Variables	I-E vs. Others		I-E vs. MC-MT		I-E vs. C-T	
	WIF	FIW	WIF	FIW	WIF	FIW
	b	*b*	*b*	*b*	*b*	*b*
Step 2: Main Effects (cont.)						
Good enough (W)	.05**	.12**	.07**	.18**	.05**	.13**
Delegation (W)	.02	-.05**	-.05*	.03	.02	-.06*
Priorities (W)	-.04*	-.06**	-.05*	-.06*	-.04	-.06*
Group	-.36**	.28**	-.35**	.22**	-.34**	.12*
Gender	-.05	.10*	-.14*	-.02	-.07	.10*
Step 3: Two-Way Interaction						
Δ*F*	4.75**	5.74**	4.33*	3.34*	4.75**	10.91**
DF	29	29	29	29	29	29
Group × Super (H)	-.14**	-.12**	-.01	-.02	-.08*	-.17**
Group × Good enough (H)	.10**	.07*	-.05	.06	.10**	.10**
Group × Delegation (H)	.01	.01	-.12*	-.07	.05	.03
Group × Priorities (H)	.05	-.01	.07	-.04	-.02	.01
Group × Super (W)	.06	.10**	-.01	.02	.07*	.13**
Group × Good enough (W)	-.024	-.09*	.02	.01	-.04	-.14**
Group × Delegation (W)	-.03	.04	-.11*	.07	-.03	.03
Group × Priorities (W)	-.03	.01	-.01	.02	-.02	-.01
Step 4: Three-Way Interaction						
Δ*F*	3.89**	3.15*	1.07	0.99	4.03**	3.08**
DF	37	37	37	37	37	37
Group × Gender × Super (H)	-.14*	-.07	.05	-.01	-.13*	-.14*
Group × Gender × Good enough (H)	.24**	.17**	.08	.11	.25**	.15*
Group × Gender × Delegation (H)	-.17**	-.16**	-.06	-.05	-.09	-.01
Group × Gender × Priorities (H)	-.06	.10	-.02	.06	-.02	.07
Group × Gender × Super (W)	.16**	.17**	.10	.04	.14*	.15*
Group × Gender × Good enough (W)	-.08	-.16**	-.10	-.10	-.08	-.16*
Group × Gender × Delegation (W)	-.01	-.07	-.09	-.05	.07	-.03
Group × Gender × Priorities (W)	-.01	.08	.01	.10	.01	-.03
*R*²	.34	.26	.33	.23	.33	.27

Note. *p < .05; **p < .01; ***p < .001; unstandardized regression coefficients are shown; I-E = Individualism-Egalitarian; MC-MT= Medium Collectivism-Medium Traditional, C-T = Collectivism-Traditional; H = Home; W= Work. For gender: 0 = male, 1 = female. For schedule of job: 0- part-time, 1-full-time. For job position: 0 = nonmanagerial, 1 = managerial.

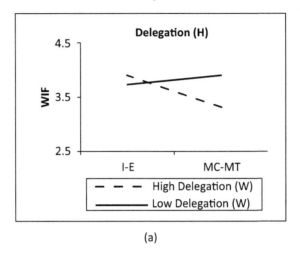

(a)

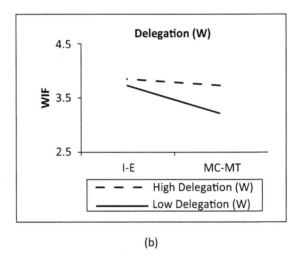

(b)

FIGURE 15.2   Interactive effect of coping strategy and group (I-E vs. MC–MT) on WIF.

entered in step 4 accounted for a further 3%. Of the eight interaction effects between group, gender, and coping strategy on WIF conflict, four were significant: *super at home* ($b = -.14, p < .05$), *good enough at home* ($b = .24, p < .001$), *delegation at home* ($b = -.17, p < .001$), and *super at work* ($b = .16, p < .001$).

The results for predicting FIW indicated that the control variables accounted for .001% of the variance in it, and the joint main effects of FIW predictors accounted for an additional 17%. The second-order interaction effects between group and coping strategy entered in step 3 accounted for an additional 6%, and

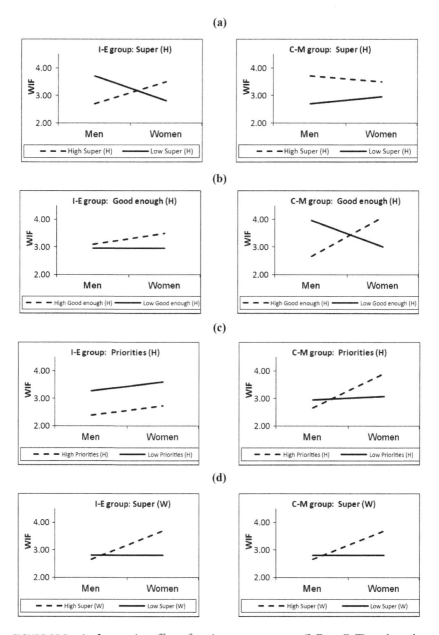

FIGURE 15.3a–d   Interactive effect of coping strategy, group (I-E vs. C-T), and gender on WIF.

the third-order interaction effects between group, gender, and coping strategy entered in step 4 accounted for a further 3%. Of the eight interaction effects between group, gender, and coping strategy on FIW, four were significant: *good enough at home* ($b = .17, p < .001$), *super at work* ($b = .17, p < .001$), *good enough at work* ($b = -.16, p < .001$), and *delegation at work* ($b = -.16, p < .001$).

To better understand the pattern of the interactions, we compared the I-E group with the MC-MT group, and the I-E group with the C-T group. Regarding the comparison between I-E group and MC-MT group, the results of the prediction of WIF indicated that the control variables accounted for .01% of the variance in it, and the joint main effects of WIF predictors accounted for an additional 26%. The second-order interaction effects between group and coping strategy entered in step 3 accounted for an additional 4%; while the third-order interaction effects between group, gender, and coping strategy entered in step 4 were not significant ($p > .05$). Of the eight interaction effects between group and coping strategy on the WIF conflict, two were significant: *delegation at home* ($b = -.12, p < .001$), and delegation at work ($b = -.11, p < .001$).

Analysis of the simple effects for the interaction between group and *delegation at home* are presented in Figure 15.2a, and revealed that for employed parents in the MC-MT group, WIF was significantly lower for those who used this coping strategy on a high than on a low level ($t = -10.3, p < .001$); however, no difference in WIF level was found for use of this coping strategy by those in the I-E group ($p > .05$). A similar pattern was found for the interaction between group and *delegation at work* (see Figure 15.2b): For the MC-MT group, WIF was significantly lower for those who used this coping strategy on a high than on a low level ($t = -9.14, p < .001$), but no difference in WIF level was found between high and low use of this coping strategy by the I-E group ($p > .05$).

The results for predicting FIW indicate that the control variables accounted for .003% of the variance in it, and the joint main effects of FIW predictors accounted for an additional 18%. The second-order interaction effects between group and coping strategy entered in step 3 accounted for an additional 4%; however, no third-order interaction effects between group, gender, and coping strategy entered in step 4 was significant. Regarding the comparison between the I-E group and the MC-MT group, the results for predicting FIW revealed no significant three-way interaction effects.

In the comparison of the I-E group with the C-T group, the results of the prediction of WIF indicated that the control variables accounted for .03% of the variance and the joint main effects of WIF predictors accounted for an additional 24%. The second-order interaction effects between group and coping strategy entered in step 3 accounted for an additional 6%, and the third-order interaction effects between group, gender, and coping strategy entered in step 4 accounted for a further 3%. Of the eight interaction effects between group, gender, and coping strategy on WIF conflict, four were significant: *super at home* ($b = -.13, p < .05$), *good enough at home* ($b = .25, p < .001$), *priorities at home* ($b = .19, p < .001$), and *super at work* ($b = .14, p < .05$).

Analysis of the simple effects revealed the following. The interaction between group, gender, and *super at home* is presented in Figure 15.3a. The results indicated that in men and women of the I-E group and in men of the C-T group, WIF was significantly higher for those who used this coping strategy on a high than on a low level ($t = 7.9, p < .001; t = 4.75, p < .0001; t = 6.63, p < .001$, respectively). However, in women of the C-T group, WIF was significantly lower for those who used this coping strategy on a high than on a low level ($t = -2.95, p < .05$).

For the interaction between group, gender, and *good enough at home* (see Figure 15.3b), in women in both groups WIF was significantly higher in those who used this coping strategy on a high than on a low level ($t = 6.58, p < .001$ for the I-E group, and $t = 8.34, p < .001$ for the C-T group). However, the relation was significantly stronger in the women of the C-T group than in the women of the I-E group. High and low use of this coping strategy by men of all groups yielded no difference between them in WIF conflict level ($p > .05$).

Next, for the interaction between group, gender and *priorities at home* (see Figure 15.3c), WIF was significantly lower in men and women of the I-E group who used this coping strategy on a high than on a low level ($t = -3.06, p < .05; t = -6.06, p < .001$, respectively); the opposite pattern was found for the women of the C-T group: WIF was significantly higher in those who used this coping strategy on a high than on a low level ($t = 3.16, p < .05$). Men of the C-T group showed no difference in WIF conflict level whether they applied high or low use of this coping strategy ($p > .05$).

As for *super at work* (Figure 15.3d), in women of both groups WIF was significantly higher in those who used this coping strategy on a high rather than on a low level ($t = 6.51, p < .001; t = 7.05, p < .001$, respectively). However, in men of the C-T group WIF was significantly lower in those who used this coping strategy on a high than on a low level ($t = -4.38, p < .05$). Men of the I-E group showed no difference in WIF conflict level whether they applied high or low use of this coping strategy ($p > .05$).

The results for predicting FIW indicate that the control variables accounted for .001% of the variance in it, and the joint main effects of FIW predictors accounted for an additional 16%. The second-order interaction effects between group and coping strategy entered in step 3 accounted for an additional 8%, and the third-order interaction effects between group, gender, and coping strategy entered in step 4 accounted for a further 3%. Of the eight interaction effects between group and coping strategy on FIW, four were significant: *good enough at home* ($b = .15, p < .05$), *priorities at home* ($b = .15, p < .05$), *super at work* ($b = .15, p < .05$), and *good enough at work* ($b = -.16, p < .05$).

Analysis of the simple effects revealed the following. The interaction effects between group, gender, and *good enough at home* are presented in Figure 15.4a. The

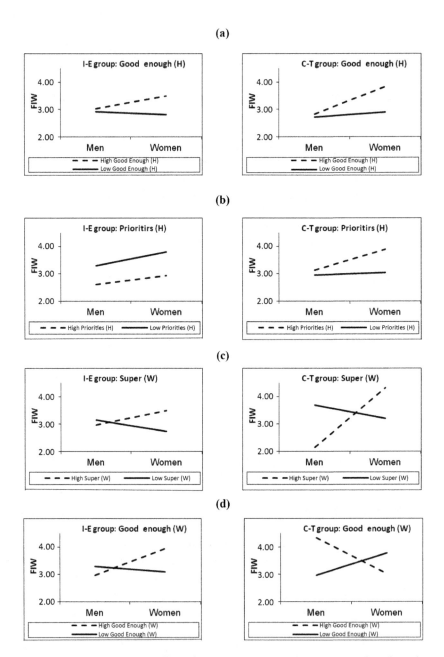

FIGURE 15.4a–d Interactive effect of coping strategy, group (I–E vs. C–T), and gender on FIW.

results indicated that in women of both groups FIW was significantly higher in those who used this coping strategy on a high than on a low level ($t = 7.09, p <$ .001 for the I-E group, and $t = 8.27, p < .001$ for the C-T group); however, the relation was significantly stronger in the C-T group than in the I-E group. Men of both groups showed no difference in FIW conflict level whether they applied high and low use of this coping strategy ($p > .05$).

For the interaction between group, gender, and *priorities at home* (see Figure 15.4b), in men and women of the I-E group FIW was significantly lower for those who used this coping strategy on a high than on a low level ($t = -6.19, p <$ .001; $t = -6.19, p < .001$); however, the opposite pattern was found in the women of the C-T group. FIW was significantly higher in those who used this coping strategy on a high than on a low level ($t = 7.30, p < .001$). The men of the C-T group showed no difference in FIW level whether they applied high or low use of this coping strategy ($p > .05$).

Next, for the interaction between group, gender, and *super at work* (Figure 15.4c), in women in both groups FIW was significantly higher for those who used this coping strategy on a high than on a low level ($t = 4.69, p < .001$ for I-E group; $t = 6.61, p < .001$ for C-T group); however, the opposite pattern was found in the men of the C-T group: FIW was significantly lower in those who used this coping strategy on a high than on a low level ($t = -4.95, p < .001$). The men of the I-E group showed no difference in FIW level whether they applied high or low use of this coping strategy ($p > .05$).

For the interaction between group and *good enough at work* (Figure 15.4d), in men and women of the I-E group and the men of the C-T group FIW was significantly higher in those who used this coping strategy on a high than on a low level ($t = 9.58, p < .001; t = 3.50, p < .05; t = 10.03, p < .001$, respectively), but the relation was significantly stronger for the men of the C-T group than for the I-E group. However, in women of the C-T group FIW was significantly lower in those who used this coping strategy on a high than on a low level ($t = -4.95$, $p < .001$).

Discussion

This chapter focused on the role of personal coping strategy in decreasing WIF and FIW taking a cross-cultural perspective, thereby contributing to bridging the gaps in knowledge of work/family issues from a cross-cultural perspective. First, our results identified distinctive patterns of coping strategies employed by individuals according to cultural differences. These findings support the notion that WFC and its related issues are inherently a cultural phenomenon (Gelfand & Knight, 2005). With respect to coping, investing in a certain set of coping strategies to ease WFC seems susceptible to values and beliefs, and might reflect social expectations and self-expectations internalized through socialization (Somech & Drach-Zahavy, 2007).

Second, we found differences between groups in level of WIF and FIW. The more individualistic/egalitarian group (I-E group) evinced a higher level of WIF than the more collectivistic/traditional groups (MC-MT and C-T); and an opposite pattern emerged regarding FIW, where the MC-MT and C-T groups reported a higher level of FIW than the I-E group. These findings can be explained on the basis of the relative values placed on family and work time in the three groups. For example, Yang et al. (2000) explained that in collectivistic cultures conceding family time for work is viewed as self-sacrifice for the benefit of the family, but in more individualistic cultures, conceding family time for work is often perceived as failure to care for significant others in one's life. Indeed, these researchers found that American employees experienced greater family demands than did Chinese employees. Spector et al. (2004) likewise found a stronger relation of number of hours worked to work-family pressure in individualist regions (Anglos) than in collectivists (Chinese and Latinos); they explained that individualists viewed working extra hours as taking time from the family while the more collectivist employees viewed working hours as a means to support the family.

Third, although all eight coping styles have the potential to reduce WFC, the main argument of the present study was that the effectiveness of certain coping styles might be universal in manner, while the usefulness of others may vary in relation to culture/group. In this study, six out of the eight coping strategies demonstrated cross-cultural differences in easing the WFC, while one strategy was more universal. We found that *priorities at work* contributed to lessening WIF and FIW across cultures, but *super at home* and *super at work*, *delegation at home* and *delegation at work*, *priorities at home*, and *good enough at home* and *good enough at work* were culture-specific. These results highlight the crucial role of culture in predicting the effectiveness of personal coping in managing WFC: when the coping strategy accords with employees' cultural values it facilitates decline in WFC.

Overall, the present results suggest that the effectiveness of a coping strategy style might depend on the congruence between cultural values and the extent of use of a certain style of coping for men and women. For those in the I-E group, in men and women alike *priorities at home* was negatively associated with WIF and FIW. But for women, *super at home* and *super at work*, and *good enough at home* were positively related to WIF, and *good enough at home* and *super at work* were associated with higher levels of FIW. In men, *super at work* was positively associated with FIW. Theoretically, these findings can be explained by the core values of high individualism and a more egalitarian gender-role ideology. Individualists view self-fulfillment and autonomy as core values, and they often reach their self-definition through their work identity; on the other hand, an egalitarian ideology means holding more even attitudes to the role of men and women at home as well at work. Moreover, research has shown that when work and family conflict, individuals in Western societies are expected to give priority to the family and to express themselves through it (Bellah, Madsen, Sullivan, Swindler, & Tipton, 1985; Yang et al., 2000). They are expected to invest time and energy at work, but because family and work are perceived as separated domains, when they do so, they feel guilt for neglecting their family duties (Lu et al., 2010). This can explain why *good enough at home* and *good enough at work* led to higher levels of WIF and FIW, while *priorities at work*, which allowed them to invest in work, but also to devote time and energy to family, led to lower levels of WIF and FIW.

For the MC-MT group, *delegation at home* and *delegation at work* were negatively associated with WIF both in men and women, but no moderating effect was found regarding FIW conflict. First, this group, which is rated in the middle of the individualism-collectivism dimension, and in the middle of the egalitarian-traditional continuum of the gender-role ideology dimension, was less distinctive than the other two groups: the I-C group (high in individualism with a more egalitarian gender-role ideology) and the C-T group (high in collectivism with a more traditional gender-role ideology). Second, the present results can seemingly be understood in the light of cultural values, but also of macro-environmental influences (Joplin, Shaffer, Francesco, & Lau, 2003). Israel and Taiwan, the two countries in the MC-MT group, have undergone fundamental transformations of industrial structures from labor intensive to high tech, as well as rapid social modernization in both work and lifestyles (Cinamon, 2009; Lu et al., 2009). These processes have caused numerous changes in these societies, especially by emphasizing a more individualistic orientation. So for people assuming an active role at work and at home, the effective strategies to handle WFC, and to balance work and family, were to delegate some of their home and work duties to others. These strategies also reflect the role of the extended families in these countries, which usually form a close-knit protective social network that can be called upon to provide support and help in time of need and distress (Lu, 2006). Delegation might be perceived as a legitimate tool to manage multiple roles, and consequently to reduce WIF.

For those in the C-T group, significant differences transpired between men and women in the effectiveness of certain strategies in decreasing WIF and FIW. In women, *super at home* was associated with a lower level of WIF, while *good enough at home*, *priorities at home*, and *super at work* were associated with a higher level of the conflict. As for the FIW, *good enough at work* was negatively associated with it, while *good enough at home*, *priorities at home*, and *super at work* were positively associated with it. For the men of the C-T group *super at work* was effective in decreasing WIF, whereas *super at home* was positively associated with it. As for FIW, *super at work* was associated with lower levels of it, and *good enough at work* was positively associated with it.

In harmony with the cultural values of the C-T group, the combination of high collectivism and traditional gender-role ideology seems to set different expectations for women and men in both the work and the family domains. The traditional gender-role ideology is gender-based, with the wife responsible for the family and the husband assuming the breadwinner's role (Higgins, Duxbury, & Lee, 1994). Accordingly, traditional women, who believe that their main role in life is to be mothers and wives, will invest most resources in the home (*super at home*) or will lessen their performance of work responsibilities (*good enough at work*) so that they can work in the paid labor force but still place family demands first, according to their gender-role attitude, hence experience less WIF. When they use coping techniques that run counter to their values and beliefs, such as setting family duties aside (*priorities at work*) or lowering the performance of family responsibilities (*good enough at home*), they will experience greater WIF. Similarly, when they try to cope with the conflict by investing extra efforts in work (*super at work*) they might experience more FIW. Regarding traditional men, who believe that family functioning is optimized when the husband specializes in market work and the wife in domestic work (Barnett & Hyde, 2001), any coping strategy that allows them to devote their time and energy to work will contribute to lowering the WFC level. Therefore, by investing the utmost effort in work demands (*super at work*) they experience lower levels of WIF. However, a coping strategy such as *super at home*, which means investing extra efforts in the home, might stand in contrast to their traditional values, hence lead to higher WIF levels (Somech & Drach-Zahavy, 2007). These results can be further supported by the collectivist values of this group. In collectivist societies, devotion to work, especially by men, is seen to be for the welfare of the family, but is also tolerated by the family. According to this family-based work ethic, extra work after official hours or on weekends is self-sacrifice for the benefit of the family rather than sacrifice of the family in the selfish pursuit of the person's own career (Lu et al., 2010; Redding, 1993). For example, Spector et al. (2004) found that Chinese demonstrated a weaker positive relation of work hours to work-family stressors than did the Anglo sample.

Limitations and Suggestions for Future Research

While the findings are encouraging for WFC research, there are methodological limitations which should be kept in mind in the interpretation of these results. First, the data were largely self-reported from one source, hence subject to bias, although research suggests that self-reported data are not as limited as was previously believed, and that people often accurately perceive their social environment (Alper, Tjosvold, & Law, 1998). Moreover, regarding workers' strain, Wright and Cropanzano (2000) argue that for any number of reasons self-report measures are and will continue to be an important information source in research. However, future research efforts should incorporate alternative designs, such as incorporating spouses' perspective. Second, the present study focused on the phenomenon of conflict that is experienced by employed parents managing work and family responsibilities; the literature attests that this experience captures only one aspect of the interplay between the two domains. This draws attention to the need to complement the focus on conflict by examining how work and family experiences enrich people's lives in general, and those of employed parents in particular, through the conceptual lens of work-family balance or positive spillover (Aryee, Srinivas, & Hwee Hoon, 2005). Third, albeit the study's focus on white-collar employees might be seen as a methodological strength of study, it is important to note that the cultural values of this subgroup might not fully represent the national cultural values. Finally, in this study we used individualism-collectivism and gender-role ideology as cultural constructs for identifying cross-cultural differences. The conflict and stress inherent in managing work and family responsibilities have proven counterbalanced by the social context. Therefore, cross-cultural research may inspire researchers to identify other cultural constructs to better understand national differences.

Summary and Conclusions

We investigated how working parents in 10 countries maneuver between work and family demands by capturing a certain repertoire of the coping strategies they used to decrease the level of WIF and FIW that they experience. Overall, our results identified distinctive patterns of coping strategies employed by individuals according to culture/group differences. These findings support the notion that the ability to cope with the stress generated from simultaneous demands of work and family is at least partially a function of the individual's capabilities, and the effectiveness of a certain coping strategy to reduce the WFC varies across cultures.

From a practical standpoint, although this study took an individual approach, the overall result that all employed parents, regardless of cultural background, reported a higher level of WIF than of FIW may imply that coping with WFC should be considered the joint responsibility of organizations and employees. Organizations may invest in intervention programs that help employees to manage conflict created by work interfering with family. First, organizational surveys might serve to single out the coping activities used by employees to deal with the variety of work and family stressors, by identifying individual differences. However, organizations, especially international and highly diverse firms, should be aware of cultural differences in how employees perceive the interplay between the two domains of work and family, and the disparate effectiveness of a certain coping strategy in easing WFC. The need for training courses or organizational change could then be determined. If necessary, organizational or training interventions could then be developed and initiated to help individuals identify, and thereafter intensify, the use of adaptive coping strategies in light of cultural differences (Havlovic & Keenan, 1991; Somech & Drach-Zahavy, 2007). However, developing an individual effective coping strategy does not mean that organizations should not be recruited to provide employees with appropriate resources to balance competing and conflicting demands from work and family domains. Organizations should clearly recognize that to "manage the situation" is part of their obligation. They should develop policies and offer benefits that might build more flexibility between work and family.

References

Alper, S., Tjosvold, D., & Law, K. S. (1998). Interdependence and controversy in group decision making: Antecedents to effective self-managing teams. *Organizational Behavior and Human Decision Processes, 74*(1), 33–52.

Aryee, S., Srinivas, E. S., & Hwee Hoon, T. (2005). Rhythms of life: Antecedents and outcomes of work-family balance in employed parents. *Journal of Applied Psychology, 90*(1), 132–146.

Barnett, R. C., & Hyde, J. S. (2001). Women, men, work and family. *American Psychologist, 56*(10), 781–796.

Behson, S. J. (2002). Coping with family-to-work conflict: The role of informal work accommodations to family. *Journal of Occupational Health Psychology, 7*, 324.

Bellah, R. N., Madsen, R., Sullivan, W. M., Swindler, A., & Tipton, S. M. (1985). *Habits of the heart: Individualism and commitment in American life.* Berkeley, CA: University of California Press.

Chun, C. A., Moos, R. H., & Cronkite, R. C. (2006). Culture: A fundamental context for the stress and coping paradigm. In P. T. P. Wong & L. C. J. Wong (Eds.), *Handbook of multicultural perspectives on stress and coping* (pp. 29–53). New York, NY: Springer.

Cinamon, R. G. (2009). Role salience, social support, and work-family conflict among Jewish and Arab female teachers in Israel. *Journal of Career Development, 36*(2), 139–158.

Firestone, J. M., Harris, R. J., & Lambert, L. C. (1999). Gender-role ideology and the gender based differences in earnings. *Journal of Family and Economic Issues, 20*, 191–215.

Folkman, S., & Moskowitz, J. T. (2004). Coping: Pitfalls and promise. *Annual Review of Psychology, 55*, 745–774.

Gelfand, M. J., & Knight, A. P. (2005). Cross-cultural perspectives on work-family conflict. In S.A.Y. Poelmans (Ed.), *Work and family: An international research perspective* (pp. 401–414). Mahwah, NJ: Lawrence Erlbaum.

Harris, R. J., & Firestone, J. M. (1998). Changes in predictors of gender-role ideologies among women: A multivariate analysis. *Sex Roles, 38*(3/4), 239–252.

Hassan, Z., Dollard, M. F., & Winefield, A. H. (2010). Work-family conflict in East vs Western countries. *International Journal of Cross Cultural Management, 17*(1), 30–49.

Havlovic, S. J., & Keenan, J. P. (1991). Coping with work stress: The influence of individual differences. *Journal of Social Behavior and Personality, 6*, 199–212.

Higgins, C., Duxbury, L., & Lee, C. (1994). Work-family conflict: A comparison by gender, family type, and perceived control. *Journal of Family Issues, 15*(3), 449–466.

Hobfoll, S. E. (1989). Conservation of resources: A new attempt at conceptualizing stress. *American Psychologist, 44*, 513–524.

Hobfoll, S. E. (2001). The influence of culture, community and the nested-self in the stress process: Advancing conservation of resources theory. *Applied Psychology: An International Review, 50*, 337–421.

Joplin, J. R. W., Shaffer, M. A., Francesco, A. M., & Lau, T. (2003). The macro-environment and work-family conflict: Development of a cross cultural comparative framework. *International Journal of Cross Cultural Management, 3*(3), 305–328.

Korabik, K., Whitehead, D. L., & Lero, D. S. (Eds.). (2008). *The handbook of work-family integration: Theories, perspectives & best practices.* New York, NY: Elsevier.

Kuo, B. C. H. (2011). Culture's consequences on coping: Theories, evidences, and dimensionalities. *Journal of Cross-Cultural Psychology, 42*(6), 1084–1100.

Lachman, M. E. (1991). Perceived control over memory aging: Developmental and intervention perspectives. *Journal of Social Issues, 47*(4), 159–175.

Lam, A. G., & Zane, N. W. (2004). Ethnic differences in coping with interpersonal stressors: A test of self-construals as cultural mediators. *Journal of Cross-Cultural Psychology, 35*, 446–459.

Lam, S. S. K., Chen, X. P., & Schaubroeck, J. (2002). Participative decision making and employee performance in different cultures: The moderating effects of allocentrism/idiocentrism and efficacy. *Academy of Management Journal, 45*(5), 905–914.

Lazarus, R. S. (1991). Psychological stress in the workplace. In P. L. Perrewé (Ed.), *Handbook on job stress* (pp. 1–13). Corte Madera, CA: Select Press.

Lazarus, R. S., & Folkman, S. (1984). *Stress, appraisal and coping*. New York, NY: Springer.

Lu, L. (2006). The transition to parenthood: Stress, resources and gender differences in a Chinese society. *Journal of Community Psychology, 34*(4), 471–488.

Lu, L., Cooper, C. L., Kao, S. F., Chang, T. T., Allen, T. D., Lapierre, L. M., O'Driscoll, M., Poelmans, S.A.Y., Sanchez, J. I., & Spector, P. E. (2010). Cross-cultural differences on work-to-family conflict and role satisfaction: A Taiwanese-British comparison. *Human Resource Management, 49*(1), 67–85.

Lu, L., Gilmour, R., Kao, S. F., & Huang, M.T. (2006). A cross-cultural study of work/family demands, work/family conflict and wellbeing: The Taiwanese vs British. *Career Development International, 11*(1), 9–27.

Lu, L., Kao, S. F., Cooper, C. L., Allen, T. D., Lapierre, L. M., O'Driscoll, M., Poelmans, S.A.Y., Sanchez, J. I., & Spector, P. E. (2009). Work resources, work-to-family conflict, and its consequences: A Taiwanese—British cross-cultural comparison. *International Journal of Stress Management, 16*(1), 25–44.

Marini, M. M., Fan, P. L., Finely, E., & Beutel, A. M. (1996). Gender and job values. *Sociology of Education, 69*, 49–65.

Parasuraman, S., Purohit, Y. S., Godshalk, V. M., & Beutell, N. J. (1996). Work and family variables, entrepreneurial career success, and psychological well-being. *Journal of Vocational Behavior, 48*, 275–300.

Redding, S. G. (1993). *The spirit of Chinese capitalism*. New York, NY: De Gruyter.

Rotondo, D. M., Carlson, D. S., & Kincaid, J. F. (2003). Coping with multiple dimensions of work-family conflict. *Personnel Review, 32*, 275–296.

Somech, A., & Drach-Zahavy, A. (2007). Strategies for coping with work-family conflict: The distinctive relationships of gender-role ideology. *Journal of Occupational Health Psychology, 12*, 1–19.

Spector, P. E., Cooper, C. L., Poelmans, S.A.Y., Allen, T. D., O'Driscoll, M., Sanchez, J. I., Siu, O. L., Dewe, P., Hart, P., & Lu, L. (2004). A cross-national comparative study of work-family stressors, working hours, and well-being: China and Latin America Versus the Anglo World. *Personnel Psychology, 57*(1), 119–142.

Thein, H. H., Austen, S., Currie, J., & Lewin, E. (2010). The impact of cultural context on the perception of work/family balance by professional women in Singapore and Hong Kong. *International Journal of Cross Cultural Management, 10*(3), 303–320.

Triandis, H. C. (1995). *Individualism and collectivism*. Boulder, CO: Westview Press.

Trompenaars, F., & Hampton-Turner, C. (1998). *Riding the waves of culture*. New York, NY: McGraw-Hill.

Wagner, J. A. (1995). Studies of individualism—collectivism: Effects on cooperation in groups. *Academy of Management Journal, 38*(1), 152–172.

Wright, T. A., & Cropanzano, R. (2000). Psychological well-being and job satisfaction as predictors of job performance. *Journal of Occupational Health Psychology, 5*, 84–94.

Yang, N., Chen, C. C., Choi, J., & Zou, Y. (2000). Sources of work-family conflict: A Sino-U.S. comparison of the effects of work and family demands. *The Academy of Management Journal, 43*(1), 113–123.

6

WORK, REST AND PLAY

The importance of brief and daily rest for employee resilience

Frances McMurtie and Dr. Monique F. Crane

The concept of work, rest and play is well known. Nearly every role imaginable has specific working hours, and traditionally, the time outside of those hours were the employees' to enjoy. However, with the introduction of the internet, and ability for people to work remotely, the boundary between work and the remainder of employees' days have become blurred. Now the average working week is no longer constrained to 40 hours Monday to Friday, and employees can be reached at any time of the day, any day of the week thanks to mobile phones and email. This might sound great from a productivity perspective. After all, what's wrong with having a workforce available at all hours of the day for the same cost as a traditional 9 to 5 role? The problem is that this way of working neglects employees' need for recovery from the strain of the workday, and this has serious implications for their personal wellbeing, and their employment performance.

Prior research shows that recovery during daily respite, such as in evenings and weekends, is associated with enhanced wellbeing, work engagement and next-day job performance (Sonnentag, 2003; Totterdell *et al.*, 1995). Conversely, failure to recover frequently from stressors leads to the chronic accumulation of stress and has implications for longer-term physical and mental health (e.g., Brosschot, Gerin & Thayer, 2006; Geurts & Sonnentag, 2006). Taken together, the above research suggests that daily respite periods are an important opportunity to facilitate psychological resilience by assisting employees regularly recover from daily work stress. Fortunately, it is not the time available for the rest that matters, but rather the *quality* of the rest experience (Westman & Eden, 1997). Given the increasingly limited time available for daily rest it is critically important to maximise the psychological benefit gained from daily respite for the management of chronic job stress. In this chapter, we will review the factors that contribute to effective recovery from work, and practical steps employers and employees can take to maximise the effectiveness of rest periods experienced by employees.

The importance of recovery and psychological detachment from work

Recovery from work refers to the process of reducing the physical, mental and emotional strain that is caused by job stressors (Craig & Cooper, 1992). This means that an individual's resources that are normally called upon during work are given time to be revived during non-work time (Meijman & Mulder, 1998; Zijlstra & Sonnentag, 2006). Research investigating how well employees are able to recover from work has demonstrated that the quality of this recovery process has important impacts on wellbeing and job-related behaviours. It may seem like common sense that time spent resting after or between work periods is beneficial and worthwhile for employees. What is less understood; however, is how this time 'recovering' from work should be spent to most effectively support an individual's wellbeing, and also their performance in their employment.

A particularly important aspect of the recovery process during leisure time appears to be psychological detachment from work. The notion of psychological detachment from work was introduced by Sonnentag and Bayer (2005) in an effort to describe ideal circumstances for recovery from work strain. Psychological detachment means that the employee is able to completely refrain from any work-related activities and not even think about job-related activities (Sonnentag & Fritz, 2015). It might be useful at this point to consider how often you are psychologically detached from your work. If psychological detachment from work is not something that you are achieving often when not physically at work then it may be the same for your employees.

Psychological detachment from work is a critical aspect of the recovery process and means more than simply not being at work. The effect of a bad day at work can impact how employees feel after the workday is complete. For example, an employee may find that if they experience a particularly stressful day at work, when they arrive home their mood will be low as a result of their difficult day. This can have carry-over effects whereby the individual may experience difficulties with their family or friends, or feel unable to effectively 'switch-off' from their difficult day as a result of their low mood. The challenge is that greater job stress is actually thought to reduce the ability to become psychologically detached from work (Sonnentag, Kuttler & Fritz, 2010). The lack of psychological detachment is then likely to mean that there is limited recovery. Experiencing an evening like this will further contribute to the employee's low mood, and will prevent them from achieving high quality recovery time from their workday. This lack of recovery will then negatively impact the employee's ability to perform well at work the following day (Sonnentag & Binnewies, 2013). Most people have probably experienced feeling worried or pre-occupied about their work after the workday is complete. You might not really engage with your family during the evening, or spend the night sleeping poorly as a result of your work worries. This is what happens when employees fail to detach effectively from work at the end of each day. Even though they are no longer at work, they continue to think about it after hours. This thinking stops them from fully engaging with their life outside of work, and from achieving effective recovery. This is a negative cycle whereby a difficult day at work can lead to a difficult night, which in turn leads to fatigue, low mood and disengagement in work the following day, and so this pattern will continue. Perhaps this is a cycle that seems familiar. It is for this reason that achieving high quality recovery time from work is incredibly important. To do so, employees must be able to successfully "detach" themselves from their workday.

There is extensive research regarding the importance of detachment from work, and how this improves employee mood and engagement after hours, and work performance the following day. Effective psychological detachment during breaks and after work has been shown to assist employees with managing job demands, and in protecting their well-being and work engagement (Sonnentag, Binnewies and Mojza, 2010). For instance, Sonnentag, Binnewies, and Mojza (2010) found that low psychological detachment from work during non-work time predicted greater emotional exhaustion over the course of one year. Hahn, Binnewies, and Haun (2012) identified that when psychological detachment over a weekend was low there was an increase in the employee's negative emotional state. Furthermore, achieving psychological detachment between or after work shifts is positively associated with employee engagement and proactive behaviour the following day (Sonnentag, 2003). The consequences of not achieving psychological detachment during work breaks are also well established. Poor psychological detachment can lead to high levels of emotional exhaustion and physical illness. These in turn can increase the need for effective recovery from work, which cannot be achieved without psychological detachment. In summary, recovery and psychological detachment from work has important benefits when it is achieved, but can lead to health and performance problems when it is not.

"But, I am always working and I am totally fine"

At this point some readers might be thinking, "but I am always working and I am totally fine!". If this is you, then it is possible that your work gives you an enormous sense of mastery, meaning, and satisfaction. These experiences are also important for wellbeing and resilience as well, but we cannot assume that our employees experience them to the same extent.

How to make rest effective

We have established so far in this chapter that: (1) rest between work periods is important for employee wellbeing and performance and (2) psychological detachment from work is necessary in order for employees to engage in effective rest. We will now look at factors that make the rest period itself effective. There are four main factors that need to be taken into account in order to optimise the effectiveness of rest: (1) enjoyment, (2) home environment, (3) work characteristics and (4) timing.

(1) Enjoyment. First, the activities undertaken during the rest period must be enjoyed by the employee. A break in and of itself is not enough, the employee must be engaged in something they personally find enjoyable to facilitate effective recovery. Interestingly, even if the employee is engaged in work-related activities during their break, if this is something they find personally enjoyable he/she will still benefit from the break period. Equally, if they engage in something typically considered to be enjoyable (i.e. social activities) but do not have a good time, this will actually negatively impact on the effectiveness of their break (Oerlemans, Bakker & Demerouti, 2014). Furthermore, it is understood that employee enjoyment in both their work and non-work activities is important for recovery. The combination of enjoyable work and enjoyable non-work activities is positively associated with high quality recovery. A combination of unpleasant and effortful work negatively impacts on an employee's quality of recovery (van Hooff *et al.*, 2011).

(2) Home environment. The home environment of the employee and in particular with whom they share their home appears to affect psychological detachment from work. Research demonstrates that ability to detach is affected by the ability of the employee's partner to also detach and achieve effective rest. In this scenario, a person may be feeling reasonably detached from their work, however when their partner arrives home from what could have been a stressful day, they will want to discuss this with the first person, and ruminate on the issues they experienced at work throughout the evening. Through this interaction, the first person is likely to reflect on their own workplace to relate their partner's stories to their own experience. In this way, if the employee's partner has difficulty detaching from their work then it is likely that this will affect the ability of the employee to also detach. What is interesting however is that when children are present in this environment, the interaction effect between the partner's failure to detach is minimised. This may be because children require their parents' attention, and thus the adults are unable to remain fixated on work for the evening and inadvertently achieve detachment (Hahn & Dormann, 2013).

It has also been shown that the activities each partner engages in after work will impact on their own and each other's ability to recover. Women who engage in more housekeeping activities after work will experience higher stress levels than if they had engaged in more social or leisure activities. However, if their spouses engage in more housekeeping than social or leisure activities, women's stress levels actually decrease (Saxbe, Repetti & Graesch, 2011), thus promoting higher recovery quality (at the expense of their partners' recovery!).

(3) Work characteristics. The impact of work characteristics on recovery requires some special attention because this is where managers can really take matters into their own hands. Research has demonstrated that the characteristics of an individual's employment also affect their ability to recover effectively. Aspects like the number of work hours, hours of overtime, and time pressure tend to reduce the capacity for psychological detachment (e.g., Burke, Koyuncu & Fiksenbaum,

2009; Kinnunen, Feldt & Siltaloppi, 2011; Sonnentag & Bayer, 2005). Moreover, jobs that are highly complex and require complex decision making or focused attention are also associated with a lack of psychological detachment (Oosthuizen, Mostert & Koekemoer, 2011). Emotional demands at work may also make detachment difficult, this includes where jobs require a display of an emotion other than the one actually felt (e.g., flight attendant) or where the role is emotionally taxing (e.g., counsellor, university employees) (Sonnentag *et al.*, 2010; Oosthuizen *et al.*, 2011). These aspects of a role are often fairly difficult to change and are likely to be intrinsic to the job-role. In these situations, as a manager it is useful to be aware that as a consequence of these factors it is likely that employees are going to be less likely to detach from work, therefore it may be prudent to focused on helping employees with their ability to detach (e.g., mindfulness training). Moreover, managers need to be more mindful of any tendencies they have to engage employees in work in non-work time (e.g., emails, phone-calls, text messaging).

In contrast to the above work characteristics, there are other characteristics that a manager is likely to have a direct impact on. Some research has identified a relationship between role ambiguity (i.e., the employee is not quite sure what their role requires) and lower detachment from work (Sonnentag & Fritz, 2007). This is more likely to be the case for those employees new to the organisation or employees who are early in their career. Social stressors like workplace interpersonal conflict are also associated with less detachment (Demsky, 2012). Moreover, work-related activities using email or phone during non-work time are also unsurprisingly related to less detachment (Park, Fritz & Jex, 2011). These are all aspects of the job role that managers can do something about. For example, role ambiguity can be managed by providing clear guidance to employees about their job-requirement, goals, role and reports. For early career or new employees this could be extended to coaching or mentorship as they become adjusted to their role and the organisation. Moreover, providing constructive feedback to employees can also help to resolve ambiguity. In terms of interpersonal conflict, managers can empower employees to address these issues by providing appropriate training in handling challenging conversations and negotiation skills. Where necessary, managers can also intervene to mediate interpersonal conflict between team members, and support them to identify and follow appropriate resolution steps that protect the interests of both parties. When it comes to establishing boundaries regarding work–related activities in the home, Park and colleagues (2011) found that a strong work team culture in favour of separating work and home life was associated with higher detachment from work. Thus, a manager can establish clear boundaries for work and non-work time.

There are also some job characteristics that can actually improve the ability to detach from work. Employees offered work-related learning and opportunities for personal development are more likely to report higher levels of recovery and relaxation (Jalonen *et al.*, 2015). Higher levels of autonomy and control over one's work can also contribute to effective recovery (Oosthuizen *et al.*, 2011). In this regard, managers can work closely with their team members to build their skills in core decision-making areas of their roles, until the employee is able to demon-strate competence in acting on their judgement alone. It is recommended that managers start small with this approach by not providing employees with direction for any given situation or task, but instead asking the employee what they themselves would do. When the employee provides their response, the manager can give them feedback if their response is not at the level of judgement required and direction can be given as needed. Once the employee is consistently responding with appropriate judgement calls, the manager can then empower the employee to apply their own judgement without first checking with the manager if their approach is correct. Some employees need support with regards to confidence in this area before they can experience role autonomy, but once established, will feel a greater sense of control and ownership of their role.

(4) Timing. The fourth factor that contributes to effective recovery is the timing of activities and breaks. In relation to activities, employees who completed activities they preferred earlier in their work shift experience higher levels of recovery (Hunter & Wu, 2015). In relation to breaks, frequent short breaks help sustain an employee's resources throughout the day. The earlier in the day they are taken, the more effective these breaks are (Hunter & Wu, 2015).

Practical strategies to help employees recover effectively

A large health services provider had a large cohort of staff who repeatedly requested structured 'Rostered Days Off' (RDOs) to be allowed, in order to counteract the perceived high potential for burn-out associated with their roles. The organisation was not in a position to pay for this, and the shift-work nature of the organisation's activities did not align well to an RDO model. When questioned about their request, the staff involved stated that they would likely use the extra day off each fortnight to complete activities such as going to the bank, taking their family members to appointments, and catching up on personal administration. Even if the organisation had been in a position to support RDOs, if this was how the employees intended to spend their extra time off, it is quite clear that no real recovery was likely to occur (unless they really enjoyed admin tasks!). Instead, the organisation would have been better placed to introduce some of the following strategies to help improve employee's recovery from work and reduce the need for additional time off each fortnight.

Education. The first step in helping employees to use their rest time effectively for recovery is to provide education about the importance of effective recovery. Without this, any policies or processes put in place to support effective recovery will not be fully understood or appreciated, and the full benefit will not be realised for the employees or the organisation. As explained throughout this chapter, recovering from work is not just about not physically being at work. Supporting employees to understand this will greatly enhance their wellbeing. An education programme could take several forms, including formal training sessions, e-learning or a mentoring programme. Whichever model is selected the recovery education programme should provide employees with the following information:

1   The importance of effective recovery for their wellbeing and employment performance
2   The importance of effective detachment from work each day
3   How to achieve effective recovery through:

   •   Engaging in enjoyable activities during time away from work
   •   Prioritising enjoyable work activities earlier in the work day
   •   Supporting family members to also effectively detach from their work day

Organisational policy and practice

Supporting effective recovery can also be achieved through organisational policy and practice. Here are some steps that an organisation can take:

Electronic sundown. To support effective detachment, organisations must look for ways to counter the ever-connectedness we now experience thanks to technology. One way to achieve this is to establish communication boundaries for employees by setting an Electronic Sundown policy, which states no work communications are to occur outside of business hours. This reduces the pressure felt by employees to always be available, and will help them to detach effectively as they will not always be waiting for the next email or phone call from their boss each evening and weekend.

Agreed after-hours communication times. If an Electronic Sundown does not suit the organisation's operating model, consider negotiating with employees about when they are willing to be reached after hours. It may be that they do not wish to be contacted in the evenings after work, but they are happy to be available for a few hours each Saturday. Establishing agreed after-hours communication times provide the employees with control over their working hours. As aforementioned, control over one's work contributes to effective recovery.

Break targets. As we have established, taking frequent breaks and engaging in enjoyable activities during breaks is imperative to effective recovery and work performance. An initiative that supports this is to establish suitable break targets for each employee. By requiring each employee to take a minimum of three effective breaks throughout the day, an organisation will benefit from their workforce's improved productivity and effectiveness in their roles, compared to if no breaks were taken. As mentioned, control is an important aspect of supporting effective recovery. It is important that break targets for each employee are established with their input. Finding out when will best suit each employee to take a break, and what enjoyable activities they will engage in during their break will respect the importance of each employee having control over their work environment.

Job crafting and career progression. A common theme throughout the research regarding effective recovery is that of enjoyment. It is important for effective recovery that employees enjoy their work, and enjoy their time away from work. Managers can aid this by supporting employees to focus on aspects of their employment they most enjoy through job crafting and career progression opportunities. This can be practically achieved through the formal performance appraisal system whereby at each review, employees are asked to specify which aspects of their role they find most enjoyable, and collaboratively set targets for the subsequent review period in these areas. Further, career progression goals can be aligned to these key areas of enjoyment for each employee, and thereby tailored to each employee's preferences.

Alternatively, if the organisation does not utilise a formal performance appraisal system, managers can support their employees to craft their role to their areas of interest and enjoyment through other means. Establishing a framework for managers to speak to their team members about what they enjoy most about their role, and minimum frequencies for these conversations to take place will provide the organisation with the information they need to offer each employee opportunities aligned to their interests and areas of enjoyment.

Accountability for recovery. It is vital that employees are supported to take responsibility for their own effective recovery, in order to ensure that any recovery oriented policies and practices are supported by the workforce. A 'buddy system' for effective recovery is one way to achieve this. This system requires each employee to be allocated or to choose a buddy. The buddies will be accountable to one another for their recovery activities each week. For example, a buddy pair may meet each week to discuss their recovery activities undertaken that week, and to agree to recovery activity goals for the week ahead. The following week, those goals can be reviewed and discussed. Moreover, group based recovery sessions are also applicable for break periods during work hours, with both relaxation and physical activities found to increase the effectiveness of time spent in recovery from work (Coffeng *et al.*, 2015).

Final thoughts

It is hoped that by understanding the high importance of effective recovery for employees, and incorporating some of these suggested strategies into the organisation managers will have the tools to support their workforce to value their rest. This in turn will protect employee wellbeing, and provide the organisation with greater levels of productivity and effectiveness.

KEY MESSAGES FROM THIS CHAPTER

- Employees who recover effectively from their workday have greater wellbeing, work engagement and performance.
- Managers play an important role in establishing a work environment that enables employees to achieve effective recovery.
- Successful recovery from work requires employees to effectively detach from their jobs.
- Effective detachment involves first disengaging from the work environment (both physical and online) and then actively engaging in an enjoyable activity.
- Regular breaks throughout the workday can also support recovery from work strain, as long as the employee achieves detachment during each break.

References

Brosschot, J. F., Gerin, W. & Thayer, J. F. (2006). The perseverative cognition hypothesis: A review of worry, prolonged stress-related activation, and health. *Journal of Psychosomatic Research, 60,* 113–124.

Burke, R. J., Koyuncu, M. & Fiksenbaum, L. (2009). Benefits of recovery after work among Turkish manufacturing managers and professionals. *Education, Business and Society: Contemporary Middle Eastern Issues, 2,* 109–122.

Coffeng, J., van Sluijs, E., Hendriksen, I., van Mechelen, W. & Boot, C. (2015). Physical activity and relaxation during and after work are independently associated with the need for recovery. *Journal of Physical Activity and Health, 12,* 109–115.

Craig, A. & Cooper, R. E. (1992). Symptoms of acute and chronic fatigue. In A. P. Smith & D. M. Jones (eds), *Handbook of human performance* (Vol. 3, pp. 289–339). London: Academic Press.

Demsky, C. A. (2012). Interpersonal conflict and employee well-being: The moderating role of recovery experiences. *Dissertations and Theses.* Paper 766.

Geurts, S. A. E. & Sonnentag, S. (2006). Recovery as an explanatory mechanism in the relation between acute stress reactions and chronic health impairment. *Scandinavian Journal of Work, Environment, and Health, 32,* 482–492.

Hahn, V., Binnewies, C. & Haun, S. (2012). The role of partners for employees' recovery during the weekend. *Journal of Vocational Behavior, 80,* 288–298.

Hahn, V. & Dormann, C. (2013). The role of partners and children for employees' psychological detachment from work and well-being. *Journal of Applied Psychology, 98,* 26–36.

Hunter, E. M. & Wu, C. (2015). Give me a better break: choosing workday break activities to maximize resource recovery. *Journal of Applied Psychology, 101,* 302–311.

Jalonen, N., Kinnunen, M.-L., Pulkkinen, L. & Kokko, K. (2015). Job skill discretion and emotion control strategies as antecedents of recovery from work. *European Journal of Work and Organizational Psychology, 24,* 389–401.

Kinnunen, U., Feldt, T., Siltaloppi, M. & Sonnentag, S. (2011). Job demands – resources model in the context of recovery: Testing recovery experiences as mediators. *European Journal of Work and Organizational Psychology, 20*, 805–832.

Meijman, T. & Mulder, G. (1998). Psychological aspects of workload. In P. J. Drenth & H. Theirry (eds), *Handbook of work and organizational psychology: Vol. 2. Work psychology* (pp. 5–33). Hove, England: Psychology Press.

Oerlemans, W. G. M., Bakker, A. B. & Demerouti, E. (2014). How feeling happy during off-job activities helps successful recovery from work: A day reconstruction study. *Work and Stress, 28*, 198–216.

Oosthuizen, J., Mostert, K. & Koekemoer, F. (2011). Job characteristics, work-nonwork interferences and the role of recovery strategies among employees in a tertiary institution. *SA Journal of Human Resource Management, 9*, 1-15, retrieved from: www.sajhrm.co.za/index.php/sajhrm/article/view/356

Park, Y., Fritz, C. & Jex, S. M. (2011). Relationships between work-home segmentation and psychological detachment from work: the role of communication technology use at home. *Journal of Occupational Health Psychology, 16*, 457–467.

Saxbe, D. E., Repetti, R. L. & Graesch, A. P. (2011). Time spent in housework and leisure: Links with parent's physiological recovery from work. *Journal of Family Psychology, 25*, 271–281.

Sonnentag, S. (2003). Recovery, work engagement, and proactive behavior: A new look at the interface between nonwork and work. *Journal of Applied Psychology, 88*, 518–528.

Sonnentag, S. & Bayer, U. (2005). Switching off mentally: predictors and consequences of psychological detachment from work during off-job time. *Journal of Occupational Health Psychology, 10*, 393–414.

Sonnentag, S. & Binnewies, C. (2013). Daily affect spillover from work to home: Detachment from work and sleep as moderators. *Journal of Vocational Behavior, 83*, 198–208.

Sonnentag, S., Binnewies, C. & Mojza, E. J. (2010). Staying well and engaged when demands are high: The role of psychological detachment. *Journal of Applied Psychology, 95*, 965–976.

Sonnentag, S. & Fritz, C. (2015). Recovery from job stress: The stressor_detachment model as an integrative framework. *Journal of Organizational Behavior, 36*, S72-S103.

Sonnentag, S. & Fritz, C. (2007). The recovery experience questionnaire: development and validation of a measure for assessing recuperation and unwinding from work. *Journal of Occupational Health Psychology, 12*, 204–221.

Sonnentag, S., Kuttler, I. & Fritz, C. (2010). Job stressors, emotional exhaustion, and need for recovery: A multi-source study on the benefits of psychological detachment. *Journal of Vocational Behavior, 76*, 355–365.

Totterdell, P., Spelten, E., Smith, L., Barton, J. & Folkard, S. (1995). Recovery from work shifts: How long does it take? *Journal of Applied Psychology, 80*, 43–57.

van Hooff, M. L. M., Geurts, S. A. E., Beckers, D. G. J. & Kompier, M. A. J. (2011). Daily recovery from work: The role of activities, effort and pleasure. *Work & Stress, 25*, 55–74.

Westman, M. & Eden, D. (1997). Effects of a respite from work on burnout: Vacation relief and fade-out. *Journal of Applied Psychology, 82*, 516–527.

Zijlstra, F. R. & Sonnentag, S. (2006). After work is done: Psychological perspectives on recovery from work. *European Journal of Work and Organizational Psychology, 15*, 129–138.

7

MANAGING AND PREVENTING EMPLOYEE BURNOUT

Edward M. Mone and Manuel London

So far, we have presented key concepts, best practices, techniques, and tools to help you drive employee engagement through effective performance management. We have focused on the positive concept of engagement and what you can do to help employees feel more engaged at work. In an ideal world, this would be sufficient; however, certain factors and conditions in the workplace can negatively affect employee engagement in your organization, and in fact can lead your employees down the opposite path—to burnout, low performance, and withdrawal. Consequently, it is crucial for you to understand burnout, including its personal and organizational consequences, its major causes, how to undo the damage (alleviate burnout and create a more engaging work environment), and how to prevent burnout. You will find that much of what we have discussed throughout this book in support of employee engagement—the concept, ideas, strategies, techniques, and so on—will be found in this chapter, and are shown to be effective in helping to prevent and eliminate burnout.

Let's begin with the following scenario:

> For the most part, you have thought of your employees as being high performing. They generally have a positive attitude and optimistic outlook. They work well together, communicate with each other frequently and clearly, and deliver effective results in a timely manner. However, recently the demands on your employees have increased. They are working harder and putting in more hours. These demands are likely to continue. You have begun to notice that the general climate in your organization is less positive. Some employees have complained about being overworked. They have missed deadlines, and the quality of their work isn't what it used to be.

Does this scenario sound familiar? Do you recognize any of these characteristics in your employees? One of the most striking findings in the literature on burnout pertains to its severity and prevalence in organizations. The leading researchers on the topic, Maslach and Leiter (1997), described burnout as a "crisis" and an "epidemic." The increasing pressures to raise the bar (do more with less, beat the competition, meet tight production deadlines, and so on) are taking their toll. Today, any one of your employees is likely to be doing the work that used to be accomplished by two or three people, working longer hours, and, given advances in technology, "staying connected" 24/7. These changes and increased pressures, in addition to the rising demands of everyday life, may leave many of your employees feeling drained and exhausted, and in some cases burned out.

According to Maslach and Leiter (1997), there has been a clear shift in the paradigm of burnout. Initial thoughts about burnout positioned it solely as an employee's problem and responsibility to address. However, current research and theory reposition burnout as being more organization driven. With this shift in emphasis, many managers have begun to ask about the actions they can take to alleviate and prevent burnout, and to ultimately develop a work environment that fosters employee engagement.

Clearly, you should be concerned about burnout, how to manage it when it occurs, and how to prevent it when possible. If you have any doubt, just consider the following adverse effects burnout can have on your employees, as well as the cumulative impact it can have on the overall success of your organization:

- Stress-related health issues (e.g., high blood pressure).
- Feelings of anxiety, depression, lower self-esteem, and so on.
- Negative impact on life at home.
- Job dissatisfaction (e.g., job is no longer challenging or exciting).
- Less enthusiasm about the organization (e.g., feeling apathetic about positive organization change).
- Negative impact on coworkers (e.g., by demonstrating cynicism, poor interpersonal relationships, etc.).
- Increased absenteeism or lateness to work.
- Reduced productivity (e.g., taking longer to complete routine assignments).
- Decreased effectiveness (e.g., not as innovative, creative, etc.).

Essentially, burnout "takes an emotional toll on the worker and it takes an economic toll on the workplace" (Maslach & Leiter, 1997, p. 154). You can, however, play an integral role in reducing the negative effects of burnout. But before you can successfully do so, you need to fully understand the construct of burnout.

What Is Burnout?

Research in general positions burnout as a physical, mental, and emotional response to chronic and prolonged levels of elevated stress. It is a state of extreme exhaustion caused by the inability to meet ongoing environmental demands such as a heavy workload, tight deadlines, and conflicting personal and professional obligations. Typically, you can associate burnout with feelings such as being exhausted, not getting anything done, being out of the loop, not caring anymore, wanting to give up, being bitter about everything, acting annoyed and angry, and showing resentment.

Although the terms *burnout* and *stress* are often used interchangeably, they are distinctly different in their characteristics and outcomes. *Stress* is a short-term emotional reaction to the demands in the environment that generally causes feelings of worry or tension. Stress is often associated with the fight-or-flight reaction—the adaptive, physiological response you would take to either fight against or attempt to escape stressful situations. Typically, these situations are not long term and can be resolved relatively quickly.

Similar to Maslach and Leiter (1997, 2000), we describe *burnout* (the opposite of employee engagement) as feeling sluggish (rather than energized), having a pessimistic outlook (vs. an optimistic outlook), and feeling ineffective (vs. enjoying a sense of personal accomplishment). Burnout is a result of continuous, chronic exposure to stress. It develops over time and has long-term consequences and outcomes. It is characterized by varying degrees of *exhaustion, cynicism,* and *ineffectiveness.* Note that your goal, as a manager, is to create a climate that safeguards employees against the possible causes of burnout and, in turn, fosters engagement.

Causes of Burnout

Burnout can be triggered by various personal, personality-centered, organizational, and work environment factors (Maslach & Leiter, 1997; Smith, Jaffe-Gill, Segal, & Segal, 2008). In Tables 10.1 and 10.2, you will find a list of personal and personality-centered factors drawn from Smith et al. (2008) as well as a number of other sources that can cause burnout. Through performance management, you may be able to affect some of these causes, such as an employee's unrealistic expectations, idealistic job and career goals, and his or her understanding of the obstacles to success. You may also be able to help your employees to increase their resilience—a personality-centered cause. Recognize, however, that most of the causes listed in Tables 10.1 and 10.2 will, by and large, need to be self-managed by your employees. Therefore, you should primarily focus your efforts on where you can make a direct impact: the organizational and work environment factors—and there are a number of these factors that could trigger burnout.

TABLE 10.1 The Personal Causes of Burnout Checklist

There are a number of personal behaviors, attributes, and reactions described below that could potentially lead to burnout over time. Being aware of these potential causes is the first step to alleviating or preventing burnout.

- *Experiencing individual changes*: Shifts in your personal beliefs, interests, values, or views of your job that conflict with your current roles and responsibilities.
- *Having unrealistic expectations*: Expecting too much of yourself; expecting too much from your job (e.g., anticipating significant opportunities or projects).
- *Having idealistic job and career goals*: Setting goals way beyond your current knowledge, skills, and abilities.
- *Having an inability to set and maintain boundaries*: Taking on too much and/or not being able to say no to requests.
- *Feeling overly responsible for low levels of personal accomplishment*: Attributing an inability to achieve goals to your own actions and not considering inevitable obstacles in your work environment.
- *Being a perfectionist*: Constantly trying to reach a level of perfection in all you do.
- *Being overly self-critical*: Consistently and regularly criticizing yourself and/or your work; holding yourself to extremely high standards.

TABLE 10.2 The Personality-Centered Causes of Burnout Checklist

Some behaviors that may contribute to burnout are often demonstrated by those who have certain personality characteristics. Although these personality characteristics have been found to be associated with burnout, keep in mind that having several of these characteristics does not necessarily mean you are burned out.

- *Having low levels of hardiness*: You typically demonstrate a low level of commitment to everyday activities (e.g., family, work, etc.), feeling like you lack control over life events and that you are being resistant to change.
- *Having low levels of resilience*: Generally you find it difficult to deal with setbacks effectively and to bounce back from challenges and stressful situations.
- *Demonstrating passive coping style*: You tend to avoid or ignore stressful situations rather than confronting them.
- *Demonstrating defensive coping style*: You usually express aggression, anger, withdrawal, and the like when faced with stress.
- *Demonstrating external locus of control*: You believe that what happens to you is beyond your control and that your behavior is guided by fate, luck, or other external circumstances.
- *Having low self-esteem*: You tend to have low confidence in your abilities and yourself overall.
- *Demonstrating type A behavior*: You can be characterized as being tense, impatient, aggressive, hostile, and time sensitive.

The Job Demands-Resources Model of Burnout

As we discussed in Chapter 4, the job demands-resources model provides us with additional insight into understanding how job demands and resources can affect engagement and burnout (Bakker and Demerouti 2007; Bakker, Demerouti, & Sanz-Vergel, 2014; Demerouti et al., 2001; Demerouti & Cropanzano, 2010; Schaufeli & Salanova, 2014). If you recall, job demands can be divided into challenges and hindrances; challenges are supportive of engagement, and hindrances can lead to burnout. Importantly, job hindrances can include role and interpersonal conflicts, emotional demands, bureaucratic barriers, and insufficient funds or staffing. Job resources have been shown to increase engagement and decrease burnout (Crawford et al., 2010); in other words, not having sufficient job resources can lead to burnout. This includes resources such as autonomy on the job, informative feedback that helps your employee improve performance, opportunities for employees to participate in making decisions, especially those that affect them, and support from you, the manager. Of course, we have previously discussed a variety of performance management actions you can take relative to job demands and job resources that foster engagement rather than contribute to employee burnout. Next, we explore additional actions you can take, particularly the importance of promoting recovery and encouraging detachment.

Recovery from a day's work can be considered a job resource (Sonnentag, Mojza, Demerouti, & Bakker, 2012). Having little time to recover can lead to stress and burnout. Feeling refreshed and recovered when your employees arrive at work can lead to engagement. However, the advantages from returning to work after a vacation or a good night's sleep will be lost quickly if your employees return to a host of frustrations. As a manager, try to limit the constraints your employees face. We provide advice for this in the upcoming section on how to address your employees' workload.

Sonnentag et al. (2012) recommend that managers help their employees detach from work to foster recovery from stress. Other research (Sonnentag, Binnewies, & Mojza, 2010) suggests it might be best for your employees to detach only in a moderate way to maintain the highest levels of job performance (Fritz, Yankelevich, Zarubin, & Barger, 2010) and to contribute, possibly, to their life satisfaction and improved work-life balance by sharing positive work experiences with their significant other at home (Ilies, Liu, Liu, & Zheng, 2017). Notably, detachment is different from disengaging. Detachment basically means not thinking about work during nonwork times, whether good (new approaches or opportunities to take) or bad (issues, concerns, problems, etc.). Not being able to detach to the extent necessary results in emotional exhaustion, a key component of burnout, while also having a negative impact on work engagement. Therefore, it pays for you to coach your employees to disengage appropriately, to ensure their ability to perform and meet your expectations.

Consider these additional actions in the context of the job demands-resources model when considering ways to help your employees cope in the face of potential burnout:

- Encourage your employees to be "mindful"—which can buffer the negative effects of job demands and resource constraints. Mindfulness is the ability to focus on the present with an attitude of acceptance (Taylor & Millear, 2016).
- Coach your employees to develop their emotional intelligence, for that helps them to seek and take advantage of social support, helping them cope with increased job demands and low job resources (Ju, Lan, Li, Feng, & You, 2015).
- Remember to act ethically and foster trust between you and your employees, as discussed in Chapter 3, for this leads to lower burnout and higher task performance (Mo & Shi, 2015).

Work Environment Factors and Burnout

Organizations, in general, are in a constant state of flux as they strive to be competitive and successful. This flux and attendant pressures are wearing on employees. Although you may not be able to personally control the impact of organizational changes and pressures on your employees, drawing from the work of Maslach and Leiter (1997), there are six specific work environment factors that you can influence:

1. *Workload*: The extent to which your employees can manage the work they have to do and feel they have the appropriate and required resources to complete the work successfully.
2. *Control*: The extent to which your employees feel a reasonable level of autonomy over their work and a sense of control over their day-to-day activities and tasks.
3. *Recognition and reward*: The extent to which your employees feel they are receiving appropriate feedback, incentives, and compensation for their performance.
4. *Community*: The extent to which your employees feel they have social support from you and their coworkers.
5. *Fairness*: The extent to which your employees feel that the larger organization's procedures and practices and those of your organization are sensible and equitable.
6. *Values*: The extent to which your employees feel their personal values coincide with the larger organization's values and those of your organization.

If your employees are not satisfied with any or all of the factors, misalignments between their needs, and those of the work environment emerge (Maslach & Leiter, 1997). Recall, too, that having the resources to do your job, getting performance feedback, being satisfied with your total rewards, and so on, as highlighted in these factors, were found to be predictors of engagement as discussed in Chapter 1.

So let's now consider each factor in more detail as it relates to burnout summarizing and building on Maslach and Leiter (1997, 2008).

Workload

Workload is the most common and understood key driver of burnout. Over time, high demands, standards and expectations, tight deadlines, consistent crises, and limited or no resources can leave your employees feeling overwhelmed and overworked. If a demanding workload is chronic and not followed by opportunities to rest and recover, it will become extremely difficult for your employees to stay engaged or sustain effective performance.

Control

Control, or feeling empowered, is critical to engagement. Remember our discussion of trust and empowerment in Chapter 3. Failing to provide your employees with high levels of autonomy, independence, and discretion in making decisions and solving problems to achieve results will inhibit their commiment, initiative and innovation, and trust. In addition, micromanaging how your employees' work gets accomplished will hinder morale and engagement and likely lead to burnout. We recognize that giving up control over outcomes for which you are accountable can be stressful. This is where self-management and balance come in. You can learn to balance the amount of autonomy you give your employees with the control you really need. This may be easier said than done. Still, it is worth the effort to maintain employee engagement.

Recognition and Reward

Lack of recognition and reward can leave your employees feeling uncertain about the quality of their performance and, much worse, devalued. These feelings can be very demotivating, leading to burnout. Ongoing positive and constructive feedback and frequent, meaningful recognition are essential to effective performance management. If you do not regularly provide feedback to your employees, you are likely sending a message that they are not worth the investment of your time and energy. Furthermore, unless you make recognition and rewards salient and tailored to your employees' needs and preferences, they may not fully value and appreciate your efforts.

Community

A poor sense of community can be detrimental to your employees' overall connection to your organization and your company as a whole. As organizations continue to become more complex and global, teamwork and collaboration become more integral to business success. If the social environment and interactions among your team members are not positive and supportive, the likelihood for burnout increases. This can be intensified if you do not treat all of your employees equitably and respectfully. The challenge is even more complex when leading a remote team. If you make little effort to regularly and consistently interact and communicate with your team members, they will feel detached, excluded, and uncertain about their connection to your organization and the company.

Fairness

Fairness is characterized by feelings of equity and balance that result when your employees weigh the time and effort they expended and the recognition and reward they received. Your employees' perceptions of fairness are driven less by the actual positive outcomes they may receive and more by how they perceive the work processes are implemented (Latham et al., 2005; Maslach & Leiter, 2008). For example, feelings of inequity can arise when your employees believe the appraisal, promotion, and reward processes are administered based on favoritism, not merit. All in all, if the sense of equity is not maintained, your employees may restore the balance by putting in less time and effort. This is likely to decrease their engagement, productivity, and performance, possibly leading to feelings of burnout.

Values

When there is a misalignment between your employees' personal values and the values held by your organization and the company as a whole, burnout is more likely to occur. For example, when an employee is asked to cover up a mistake or stretch the truth to make a sale, this could potentially cause a clash in values. Persistent value clashes can lead to deep intrapersonal conflict and a lack of engagement.

In summary, you can limit or prevent burnout by managing employees' workloads, ensuring they have the control they need to do their jobs, giving them recognition for excellent performance, building a sense of community in the team, treating them fairly, and making sure that you communicate values that they share.

Identifying Burnout

Because the effects of burnout are exhibited in unique ways, how can you determine if one of your employees is experiencing burnout? Although there is not an exact formula, there are common signs and symptoms that you can recognize. Generally the more signs and/or symptoms one of your employees is experiencing, the more likely he or she could be burned out, or close to it.

Early Warning Signs of Burnout

There is a range of feelings your employees will typically describe prior to their actually becoming burned out:

- Powerlessness.
- Hopelessness.
- Drained.
- Frustrated.
- Detached from people and things around them.
- That their work is not meaningful.
- Resentful of having too much to do.
- Like a failure.
- Stuck in a situation and feeling there is no way out.
- Withdrawn and isolated from coworkers and friends.
- Insecure about their competence and abilities.
- Cynical.
- Irritable.
- Anxious.

You may not have insight into the degree to which any of your employees is having these feelings. This is why an open and trusting relationship with your employees is a critical prerequisite to understanding how they are feeling (see our discussion of trust in Chapter 3). In other words, without high levels of trust, your employees may never tell you what they may be experiencing.

Symptoms of Burnout

Symptoms of burnout fall into three basic categories: psychological symptoms, physical symptoms, and behavioral symptoms (Maslach & Leiter, 2008; Smith et al., 2008). The psychological and physical symptoms may be harder for you to detect unless you have a trusting relationship with your employees. However, this does not mean you will not see these symptoms; it just means that they may not be as obvious as the behavioral symptoms likely are. For example, psychological symptoms of burnout include loss of care and concern, feeling apathetic, expressions of cynicism and negativity, and an inability to make decisions. Physical symptoms include exhaustion, fatigue, or changes in weight. Appendix 10.1 includes expanded lists of the psychological, physical, and behavioral symptoms of burnout.

The behavioral symptoms of burnout will likely be the most obvious to you, and the most apparent of those include:

- Decreased job performance.
- Loss of enthusiasm for the work.
- Increased frustration with the job.
- Decreased desire to communicate.
- Tendency to withdraw.
- Tardiness.
- Poor concentration and/or difficulty focusing.
- Forgetfulness.
- Accident proneness.

Overall, the rule of thumb for identifying these symptoms of burnout is to look for unfavorable changes in your employees' behavior.

Although your employees may not have come to you with concerns of being burned out, this does not mean that burnout is not a problem. Getting to know the needs and wants of your employees, their typical performance, and their work behavior patterns, as well as becoming aware of, and sensitized to, the burnout signs and symptoms, will help you to recognize and act on any potential changes in employee engagement and performance.

Taking Action to Reduce Burnout

As a manager, you have an essential role in minimizing and preventing employee burnout. The best way to do this is through a collaborative effort with your employees (Maslach & Leiter, 1997). First, let's look at the major strategies your employees can use to alleviate any signs or symptoms of burnout they may be experiencing. These strategies include:

- Practicing effective time management.
- Taking breaks.
- Setting realistic goals.
- Eating well.
- Exercising.
- Communicating with you, their manager, when they feel overwhelmed and/or unrewarded.

You may be thinking that these strategies seem rather simplistic. But if practiced regularly, they can have a profound impact on your employees' health and well-being. Therefore, although these are employee-driven strategies, we recommend that you become familiar with them (see Appendix 10.2 for an expanded and detailed list of strategies, and Appendix 10.3 for a list of tactics to address personality-centered causes of stress). Suggest or recommend these strategies to your employees, as appropriate.

As a manager, you need to determine which work environment factors are having an unfavorable effect on your employees so that you can focus your efforts where they will have the greatest impact. The best way to do this is by talking to your employees—advice we offered earlier. Discover how they feel and what they think. Once you have identified the work environment factors that are causing burnout, work collaboratively with your employees to determine the most appropriate actions. You have to think creatively and capitalize on performance management to essentially do what works best for you and your team.

Drawing from and expanding on Maslach and Leiter (1997, 2008) and Leiter and Maslach (2005), let us now take a deeper look at each factor and consider how you can minimize burnout and maximize employee engagement through effective performance management.

Addressing Workload

Workload is something you can directly impact through good performance management. An essential part of your manager role is structuring jobs so that the work gets done effectively and efficiently and that the most appropriate people are doing the work. This alignment usually takes place during goal setting, when you can adapt the workload to each of your employee's knowledge, skills, and abilities. Further, it is important to ensure availability of adequate and appropriate resources. With effective goal setting, your employees will be able to manage their workloads and become more successful in their jobs.

Managing workload becomes especially important when there are crises to address or when your employees are forced to "fight fires" rather than think more strategically and plan their working time. Burnout becomes a concern when the high-stress, crisis management nature of work becomes chronic and presents little to no opportunities to rest and recover. You may want to consider offering your employees days off following a major deadline or completion of a project. The need to restore balance and have sufficient opportunities to rest after a stressful period at work is critical to promoting engagement and eliminating or preventing burnout.

Addressing Control

Your employees want to have accountability for the work they do and how they do it. Further, they want to be able to solve their own problems and make decisions. It is your job to ensure your employees are empowered and provided with appropriate levels of independence and discretion. Empowering your employees plays a key role in building trust and fostering engagement. Here are some ways to avoid micromanaging the efforts of your employees:

- Do not set policies and practices that are unnecessarily rigid.
- Focus on managing the "big picture" rather than on managing the day-to-day tactical activities.
- Delegate assignments.
- Trust and empower your employees to deliver results and provide guidance, as needed.
- Offer flexibility in the way work gets done.

Your employees will feel more empowered and engaged when they have the opportunity to feel ownership of their performance and results and they recognize how their contributions directly support the goals of the team and the organization.

What are some other steps you can take to ensure you are empowering your employees, demonstrating your trust and confidence in them, and letting them drive their own performance? Consider these few suggestions in addition to those discussed in Chapter 3:

- Bring your employees together to develop and agree to the appropriate levels of decision making and authority.
- Clarify with each employee his or her areas of decision-making responsibility.
- Spell out the range and depth of authority each employee has—set the boundaries and make them clear.
- Ask your employees about the level of involvement they want from you, agree to it, and follow through.
- Ask what you can do to be helpful, but do not usurp your employees' authority, once it is granted.
- When your employees come to you with problems or opportunities, ask for their recommended plan of action and avoid the urge to provide "the answer."

You might also want to consider creating a detailed empowerment plan for each of your employees using the planning tool presented in Chapter 3.

Addressing Recognition and Reward

An integral part of effective performance management is providing your employees with recognition and reward for their performance and development. Recognition and reward are critical to employee engagement, as found in our study at XINC, and they enhance satisfaction, motivation, and morale, as well as sustain effective performance. Essentially, recognition and reward are forms of feedback. One of the most stressful circumstances for your employees is not knowing how their work is perceived by you. Without appropriate amounts of positive and constructive feedback as well as recognition and reward, your employees will generally begin to doubt their competence, feel devalued, and, as a result, reduce their effort. Of course, refer back to Chapter 6 to help you determine the recognition and reward strategies that will work best given your needs and the needs of your employees, and to Chapter 5 for making your feedback as effective as possible.

Addressing Community

A strong sense of community fosters greater levels of satisfaction and engagement, creating a work environment that allows your employees to perform to the best of their abilities. Essentially, if your employees have feelings of abandonment, isolation, conflict, or tension, it will have a negative impact on their satisfaction and engagement, and quite possibly lead to signs or symptoms of burnout over time.

The following ways to build a strong sense of community for your employees rests on a foundation of trust and empowerment:

- Demonstrate ongoing support in all performance and development efforts.
- Defend your employees when necessary or appropriate.
- Treat your employees equally.
- Foster an environment of mutual respect.
- Encourage ongoing relationships among your employees.
- Develop opportunities for open and supportive communication.
- Solicit and act upon your employees' ideas and opinions.

Interestingly, creating a strong sense of community can help you to mitigate the negative impact of the other five workplace environment factors (Maslach & Leiter, 2008). For example, when a team of your employees has to deliver a critical project in a short time frame, in addition to managing their day-to-day responsibilities (creating an overwhelming workload), providing your support and promoting a high degree of teamwork and collaboration will likely ease any potential feelings related to burnout. Essentially, your employees will feel that "they're not in it alone."

Urging your employees to take regular breaks and have some "fun" is another important way to promote a strong feeling of community that helps create opportunities for restoration. Consult with your teams to identify what fun events and activities they would like, while taking into consideration what is acceptable in your corporate culture. Ultimately, you will have to use your best judgment, determine the practicality of employees' suggestions, and begin incorporating them into the day-to-day routine. Be sure to seek feedback on the effectiveness of the events and offer variety to ensure your employees are satisfied and remain engaged.

Addressing Fairness

Being fair and equitable when managing your employees' performance is critical to creating an engaging work environment. Treating your employees with fairness may seem like common sense—we all know we should avoid demonstrating favoritism, applying policies and guidelines unequally, and giving unjustified recognition and rewards. However, sometimes we do not *see* that we may be demonstrating behaviors that could be perceived as unfair. The fact is that research on burnout has shown that this particular work environment factor is the key "tipping point" for experiencing burnout in the workplace (Maslach & Leiter, 2008). If your employees are showing early warning signs of being burned out due to other factors, perceiving the work environment as unequal and unfair could magnify their signs or symptoms and lead to burnout. Remember, too, that treating your employees unequally will diminish the trust they have in you.

What should you do to determine if your employees feel they are treated fairly? Solicit your employees' thoughts on their perceptions of fairness within your organization. You can do this informally or with the help of your HR partner using interviews, focus groups, or an anonymous survey, similar to the Trust and Empowerment Climate Assessment Survey described in Chapter 3.

Overall, keep the following suggestions in mind to ensure that you are managing your team members fairly and fostering a sense of engagement among all of your employees:

- Treat them with respect.
- Treat them equally, avoiding even the appearance of favoritism.
- Make just, fair, and performance-driven decisions regarding workload, levels of independence and discretion, merit increases, and other rewards.
- Extend key opportunities to those who are deserving, and make the justifications clear.
- Follow all organizational policies and guidelines—do not make exceptions for some employees and not others.
- Incorporate your employees' viewpoints when developing or reviewing organizational policies to ensure feelings of fairness.

Addressing Values

> Values are the ideals and motivations that originally attracted people to their jobs, and thus they are the motivating connection between the worker and the workplace, which goes beyond the utilitarian exchange of time for money or advancement.
>
> (Maslach & Leiter, 2008, p. 501)

Here are some ways you can increase the alignment between your employees' values, your organization's values, and corporate values:

- Help your employees understand the company's core values and how these values apply to them.
- Also help your employees to understand your organization's values; how they align to the corporate values, if different; and how these values align with their own values.
- Ask your employees how, as their manager, you impact the dynamics, current values, and work ethics of the organization and what changes they would like to see.
- Engage in ongoing discussions with your employees to ensure that their personal values remain aligned with your organization's values.
- When interviewing potential job candidates, be sure to provide a realistic job preview and describe the climate, culture, and values of your organization and the company as a whole—checking for the candidates' values and alignment.

Gaining an awareness and understanding of your employees' values, and the extent to which they are aligned with the organization's overall values, will be important to your success in preventing burnout.

In summary, you may have noticed a common theme throughout our discussion of how to address the work environment factors to alleviate burnout in your organization: two-way and continuous communication. As mentioned earlier, creating an engaging work environment requires a collaborative effort between you and your employees, and communication is central to effectively working together. We recommend that you collaborate with your employees, using the Work Environment Checklist in Appendix 10.4, to determine the necessary actions both you and your employees can take to ensure the work environment is supportive of, and fosters, employee engagement.

Thus far, we have focused on how to alleviate the signs and symptoms of burnout, so let us take a look at a more proactive approach, prevention.

Preventing Burnout

At one point or another, you have probably heard the sports idiom "The best defense is a good offense." When you think about this expression in the context of burnout, the importance of proactively managing burnout becomes clear: The best way to manage burnout is not just to alleviate it (defense), but also to prevent it in the first place (offense). As a manager, it is imperative that you take preventative measures that will ensure burnout does not become a widespread issue for your employees and, in turn, your organization as a whole.

How can you do this? The first step probably comes as no surprise: Communicate and work openly with your employees. Understanding the unique needs of each of your employees will help you create the structure and opportunities that will promote employee engagement and prevent burnout. For example, if time management is an issue for your employees, consider online or instructor-led courses, self-help books, and the like. Suggest these educational opportunities as a way of helping your employees gain the necessary knowledge and skills, and, in turn, helping them cope with stress and burnout. In addition, we encourage you to share the following tips with your employees to help them avoid burnout:

- *Keep perspective*: "Don't sweat the small stuff." Try not to let the little things lead you offtrack; concentrate on attaining your goals.
- *Set priorities*: Focus on the tasks that need immediate attention.
- *Be flexible*: As things come up, allow yourself to make adjustments in your schedule.
- *Build in buffers*: Schedule enough time to switch from one task to another in case a task takes longer than anticipated.
- *Stay in touch*: Make time for friends and family.
- *Fuel your creativity*: Find a hobby or a nonwork-related activity outside of work that helps you relax and think without pressure.

Conclusion

Your employees are your greatest corporate asset, and unless you help foster an engaging work environment by taking action against burnout, your employees' morale will deteriorate and their commitment and productivity will dwindle. Driving employee engagement through effective performance management takes effort and time, but with ongoing communication, consideration of each employee's individual needs, and collaborative persistence, you will see significant results.

If you are currently on the verge of (or experiencing) burnout, implement the strategies and actions for yourself. Be a role model for your team by managing or preventing your own burnout and maximizing your own engagement. In addition, remember that the appendixes to this chapter (Appendixes 10.1–10.4) have tools, checklists, and assessments that will help you structure your own thoughts and conversations with your employees. These resources are intended to stimulate your thinking. You will have to consider your organization, your work environment, your current projects, and the unique needs of your employees and then decide the possible strategies and actions that will be the best, most appropriate steps toward alleviating and preventing burnout, and driving employee engagement.

Appendix 10.1: Symptoms of Burnout Checklist

Burnout symptoms	The specific symptoms that individuals who are burned out generally experience can be grouped into three basic categories: • Psychological symptoms. • Physical symptoms. • Behavioral symptoms.

As you read through each list of symptoms, consider the extent to which you are currently experiencing them, and focus on those that have recently developed or increased in severity.

Assessing psychological symptoms	Psychological symptoms are expressed in an individual's attitudes and feelings. ☑ *Check all symptoms you are currently experiencing, focusing on those that have recently developed or increased in severity*: ☐ Rigidity to change/loss of flexibility. ☐ Loss of care and concern. ☐ Feeling apathetic. ☐ Cynicism/negativism. ☐ Emotional exhaustion/loss of emotional control. ☐ Low morale. ☐ Loss of patience. ☐ Inability to cope with unwanted stress. ☐ Feelings of anger/bitterness/disgust. ☐ Feelings of guilt/failure. ☐ Low confidence and satisfaction with yourself. ☐ Loss of idealism (disillusioned). ☐ Inability to make decisions. ☐ Suspicion/paranoia. ☐ Depression. ☐ Alienation. ☐ Increased worry. ☐ Overly confident/taking unusually high risks. ☐ Feeling obligated to satisfy the needs of all people at all times. ☐ Loss of charisma.
Assessing physical symptoms	Physical symptoms are actual changes in physiological functions. ☑ *Check all symptoms you are currently experiencing, focusing on those not related to a previously diagnosed health condition (although this previously diagnosed health condition may be exacerbated by burnout)*: ☐ Physical exhaustion/fatigue. ☐ Change in sleep patterns; insomnia or sleeping more than usual. ☐ Headaches. ☐ Gastrointestinal problems. ☐ Lingering/frequent colds/flu. ☐ Weight loss/gain. ☐ Shortness of breath.

continued . . .

Appendix 10.1: Continued

	☐ Hypertension.
	☐ Impaired speech.
	☐ Teeth grinding.

Assessing behavioral symptoms	Behavioral symptoms are actions or behaviors demonstrated as a result of burnout.
	☑ *Check all symptoms you are currently demonstrating, focusing on those that have recently developed or increased in severity:*
	☐ Decreased job performance/decreased job satisfaction.
	☐ Decreased desire to communicate.
	☐ Tendency to withdraw.
	☐ Desire to leave your job.
	☐ Decreased desire to come to work.
	☐ Loss of enthusiasm for your job.
	☐ Increased prescription drug or alcohol use.
	☐ Increased marital or family conflict.
	☐ Difficulty focusing on your job.
	☐ Accident proneness.
	☐ Increased frustration with your job.
	☐ Forgetfulness/poor concentration.

Appendix 10.2: Strategies for Coping with and Preventing Burnout Checklist

Psychological strategies	If you have been experiencing any of the psychological symptoms of burnout, consider the following strategies.

☑ *Check each strategy that you plan to implement:*

☐ *Give yourself time alone:* Regularly set aside some alone time to do something you truly enjoy (e.g., reading a novel, watching a movie, painting, etc.)—make it routine.

☐ *Give yourself breaks:* Take regular 5- to 10-minute breaks to get away from your desk—leave the vicinity of where you do your work. For example, go for a walk outside to clear and revitalize your mind. When traveling on business, take some time to relax and engage in recreational activities.

☐ *Set realistic goals:* Set work and personal goals (short and long term) that are specific, meaningful, and attainable, and establish a plan to maximize success and minimize the stress associated with failure.

☐ *Increase your self-awareness:* Deepen your understanding of your strengths and weaknesses; this will enable you to develop more effective coping strategies for dealing with stressful situations.

☐ *Practice efficient time management:* Develop your time management skills (e.g., construct a daily to-do list, determine your most productive time of day, and adapt your tasks accordingly) to help you establish better life balance.

☐ *Take a positive perspective:* Look at stressful times as opportunities for you to grow personally and professionally.

☐ *Take a step back from the experience:* Take time to reflect upon your experiences; consider what you can learn from them.

☐ *Stop, think, and then act:* Whenever you're panicked, feel out of control, or are facing a crisis, use the scuba diver's motto: Stop, think, and then act—take a few minutes to stop what you are doing, create an action plan, and then implement the plan. This can help prevent you from doing something you may regret.

☐ *Monitor depression:* If you have a history of depression, monitor your symptoms because burnout could cause a recurrence—consult your doctor if any signs of depression resurface.

Physical Strategies	If you have been experiencing any of the physical symptoms of burnout discussed earlier, consider the following strategies.

☑ *Check each strategy that you plan to implement*

☐ *See your doctor:* Make an appointment for a complete physical, and be prepared to discuss your concerns and symptoms related to burnout. It may be helpful to make a list of all the questions that need to be addressed ahead of time so you don't lose the opportunity for professional advice.

☐ *Sleep:* Ensure you attain the amount of sleep you need to perform each day effectively. If you have a difficult time

continued . . .

Appendix 10.2: Continued

letting go of the day's events or tomorrow's to-do list, examine your routine activities that take place an hour before you go to bed. For example, if you watch intense TV programs or work right up until you lay down, try reading a novel or listening to soothing music instead. Also, try to go to bed at the same time each night—this routine will help you fall asleep faster.

☐ *Breathe*: Close your eyes and concentrate on each breath. Control every breath as you inhale and exhale until you are breathing properly—this will help you relax.

☐ *Exercise*: Increase your physical activity to gain both short- and long-term health benefits. It can be as simple as stretching, taking a brisk walk, taking yoga classes, or briefly working out in a gym.

☐ *Eat right*: Follow a well-balanced diet to ensure you obtain the proper nutrients required to provide enough energy for your day. Eating well has a major effect on how you can properly defend yourself against the stress your body is not equipped to handle.

☐ *Laugh*: Humor can give you a more lighthearted perspective and help you view stressful events as opportunities to learn and grow, making them less threatening and more positive. Laughter brings the focus away from anger, guilt, stress, and negative emotions.

Social Strategies	In addition to developing strategies for the psychological and physical symptoms of burnout, regular and positive social interaction will help you gain a better sense of balance in your life. Consider the following strategies. ☑ *Check each strategy that you plan to implement* ☐ *Nurture your closest relationships*: Your family and friends can give you support and encouragement. Be sure to give these relationships the attention they deserve. ☐ *Expand your social network*: Become active in your community, or join a group that is personally meaningful. ☐ *Communicate your concerns about your job*: Talk to your manager or HR representative, and explore options for addressing your concerns. ☐ *Revisit job and career interests*: Take the time to talk to your manager or HR representative about your current job and career goals—ensure you are satisfied with your job/career and that you are on the right track, and make any necessary adjustments. ☐ *Practice healthy communication*: Seek out a good listener (e.g., someone who will not judge you), and share your feelings in a professional and constructive manner. ☐ *Learn to say no tactfully*: Explain your position clearly, and articulate your inability to accomplish a task effectively, given the amount of work you are already committed to completing for current tasks.

Appendix 10.3: Tactics for Addressing Personality-Centered Causes of Stress

Resiliency	Resiliency is the ability to bounce back from challenges and stressful situations. ☑ *Check the box below if you plan to increase your resiliency:* ☐ *To increase your resiliency:* 1. *Network and make social connections:* Developing close relationships with friends, relatives, community group members, and so on can contribute to a sense of well-being. 2. *View challenges as opportunities to grow:* Try to look beyond the problem, focus on the future, and gain strength from your experiences; leverage lessons learned. 3. *Accept that change is a part of life:* Embrace change to help you make the most of opportunities and challenges brought about by change. 4. *Work toward your goals:* Establish a plan, and take steps toward achieving your goals. 5. *Take action:* Be proactive in your day-to-day activities to help you move toward your goals and to help give you a sense of accomplishment. 6. *Reflect upon your experiences:* Look for opportunities for self-discovery. Think about your behavior, reactions, feelings, and the like; how they influence the outcome of your experiences; and, as a result, what you might like to change in the future. 7. *Keep things in perspective:* Try to see roadblocks and setbacks in the context of the "big picture." Face them, work toward overcoming them, and move on. 8. *Take good care of yourself:* Eat well, exercise, be positive, and spend time with friends and family.
Hardiness	Hardiness is a set of personality characteristics that support your resistance to stress. ☑ *Check the box below if you plan to increase your hardiness:* ☐ *To increase your hardiness:* 1. *Gain control:* Make changes that will help you establish a better sense of balance in your life and increase your control overall. 2. *Be committed:* Reestablish and sustain your commitment to people, your work goals, and your values. 3. *Embrace change:* See unexpected change as a positive opportunity rather than as an obstacle.
Coping style	Proactively coping is an effective strategy for handling the stressors you encounter. ☑ *Check the box below if you plan to improve your coping skills:* ☐ *To improve your coping skills:* 1. *Be assertive:* Face, and directly deal with, the issues that are stressful for you.

continued . . .

Appendix 10.3: Continued

	2. *Be proactive*: Implement some of the strategies discussed earlier to help you better cope, for example: – Discover what relaxes you, and have fun each day. – Take good care of your health. – Stay physically active. – Develop strong and supportive relationships. – Build your self-esteem. 3. *Be optimistic*: Try to see negative events as minor setbacks to be easily overcome and positive events as evidence of further success and achievement.
Locus of control	An internal locus of control is expressed when you feel that what happens to you is under your control and the outcomes are a result of your personal effort and ability. ☑ *Check the box below if you plan to develop a more internal locus of control*: ☐ *Develop a more internal locus of control*: 1. *Raise your self-awareness*: Learn more about yourself and leverage your strengths. 2. *Take accountability for your actions and behaviors*: This can help you feel more empowered and autonomous. 3. *Gain control*: Analyze situations in which you feel you lack control, and determine what you could do differently in the future to exert more control over these situations. 4. *Develop a strong understanding of your influence in situations or events*: Focus on the cause-and-effect relationship of your actions and behaviors. 5. *Recognize and celebrate small successes*: Reflect on each success and how you achieved it to develop a stronger sense of how you personally controlled the situation and outcome.
Self-esteem	Self-esteem refers to your confidence in your own worth or ability and is key to your happiness and well-being. ☑ *Check the box below if you plan to increase your self-esteem*: ☐ *Increase your self-esteem*: 1. *Empower yourself*: Let others know what you want and how you feel. 2. *Reward yourself*: Celebrate your accomplishments when you succeed. 3. *Clarify*: Ask for clarification to avoid any misunderstandings and unfavorable consequences. 4. *Ask for feedback*: Seek positive feedback about your efforts to learn more about your strengths. 5. *Build supportive relationships*: Surround yourself with people who are optimistic and encouraging. 6. *Be nice to yourself*: Treat yourself well, and do things you enjoy. 7. *Have no worries*: Face your fears, and work to overcome them. 8. *Try not to dwell on your mistakes*: Learn from these mistakes, and try not to repeat them.

Appendix 10.4: Creating a More Engaging Work Environment

Here, we build on Maslach and Leiter (1997) and Leiter and Maslach (2005) and recommend actions you can take to create a more engaging work environment categorized by each of the work environment factors. Focus on the actions associated with the factors you have identified as areas to address with your team.

Ideally you will collaborate with your employees to identify realistic solutions and strategies that will create a more engaging work environment. However, keep in mind that some changes many not be possible within your given environment.

Work with your employees to check each action you plan to implement in the Actions for Employees and Actions for Managers columns.

Factors	Actions for Employees	Actions for Managers
Workload	☐ Talk with your manager if you feel overwhelmed by your workload ☐ Request necessary resources ☐ Seek short-term help from your coworkers ☐ Enroll in training to improve your time management skills and functional skills	☐ Adapt workload to each of your employee's knowledge, skills, and abilities during goal setting ☐ Ensure availability of adequate and appropriate resources ☐ Offer your employees additional days off following a major deadline or completion of a project
Control	☐ Discuss with your manager options for increasing your autonomy ☐ Be aware of who makes decisions and for what they are accountable ☐ Seek opportunities to express your opinions and ideas ☐ Take the initiative to solve problems that arise	☐ Avoid setting policies and practices that, in effect, are too rigid ☐ Offer flexibility in the way work gets done ☐ Specify who is accountable for what actions and delegate appropriately ☐ Clarify decision-making responsibility with each of your employees ☐ Empower your employees to solve their own problems
Recognition & reward	☐ Communicate to your manager what feedback you would like to receive and how often ☐ Communicate to your manager what motivates you and what types of	☐ Recognize valued actions by providing positive feedback ☐ Utilize formal or informal ways to reward your employees, if warranted ☐ Offer constructive feedback, when appropriate

continued . . .

Appendix 10.4: Continued

	rewards mean the most to you ☐ Suggest fun recognition programs (e.g., company-paid lunch for successful performance) ☐ Discuss any concerns about your recognition and rewards with your manager	☐ Appropriately compensate your employees, if possible, based on internal and external market data
Community	☐ Develop and sustain relationships with your coworkers ☐ Enroll in training regarding building relationships with your coworkers ☐ Always express respect for others ☐ Raise concerns about feeling secluded or distant from your coworkers with your manager ☐ Engage in open and supportive communication with your manager and coworkers ☐ Suggest out-of-office social activities	☐ Demonstrate ongoing support in all performance and development efforts ☐ Encourage ongoing relationships among your employees ☐ Treat your employees equally and foster an environment of mutual respect and trust ☐ Develop opportunities for open and supportive communication with and among your employees ☐ Solicit and act on your employees' ideas and opinions ☐ Defend your employees when necessary or appropriate ☐ Encourage your employees to regularly take breaks and have fun
Fairness	☐ Treat your coworkers and your manager with respect ☐ Discuss any apparent signs of "favoritism" ☐ Constructively express your discontent regarding organizational policies	☐ Treat your employees with respect ☐ Make decisions that are just, fair and performance-driven ☐ Treat all of your employees equally; don't demonstrate "favoritism" ☐ Follow all organization policies and guidelines—do not make exceptions for certain employees and not others ☐ Extend key opportunities to those who are deserving and make the justifications clear ☐ Incorporate your employees' viewpoints when developing/reviewing organizational policies to ensure feelings of fairness

Appendix 10.4: Continued

Values	☐ Explore ways of aligning your personal values with those of the organization ☐ Discuss with your manager how you feel about the dynamics, current values and work ethics of the team and what changes you would like to see	☐ Help your employees understand the organization's values and how these values apply to them ☐ Ask your employees how you impact the dynamics, current values and work ethics of the team and what changes they would like to see ☐ Engage in ongoing discussions with your employees to ensure that their personal values are still aligned to the work environment and organization ☐ When interviewing potential job candidates, provide a realistic job preview and describe the climate, culture, and values of the team and organization

References

Bakker, A. B. & E. Demerouti (2007), The Job Demands–Resources Model: State of the Art. *Journal of Managerial Psychology*, 22(3), 309–328.

Bakker, A. B., Demerouti, E., & Sanz-Vergel, A. I. (2014). Burnout and work engagement: The JD-R approach. *Annual Review of Organizational Psychology and Organizational Behavior*, 1, 389–411. http://dx.doi.org/10.1146/annurev-orgpsych-031413-091235

Crawford, E. R., LePine, J. A., & Rich, B. L. (2010). Linking job demands and resources to employee engagement and burnout: A theoretical extension and meta-analytic test. *Journal of Applied Psychology*, 95(5), 834–848.

Demerouti, E., Bakker, A. B., Nachreiner, F., & Schaufeli, W. B. (2001). The job demands-resources model of burnout. *Journal of Applied Psychology*, 86, 499–551.

Demerouti, E., & Cropanzano, R. (2010). From thought to action: Employee work engagement and job performance. In A. B. Bakker & M. P. Leiter (Eds.), *Work engagement: A handbook of essential theory and research* (pp. 147–163). New York, NY: Psychology Press.

Fritz, C., Yankelevich, M., Zarubin, A., and Barger, P. (2010). Happy, healthy and productive: The role of detachment from work during nonwork hours. *Journal of Applied Psychology*, 95, 977–983.

Ilies, R., Liu, X., Liu, Y, Zheng, X. (2017). Why do employees have better family lives when they are highly engaged at work? *Journal of Applied Psychology*, 102(6), 956–970.

Ju, C., Lan, J., Li, Y., Feng, W., & You, X. (2015). The mediating role of workplace social support on the relationship between trait emotional intelligence and teacher burnout. *Teaching and Teacher Education*, 51, 58–67. https://doi.org/10.1016/j.tate.2015.06.001

Latham, G. P., Almost, J., Mann, S., & Moore, C. (2005). New developments in performance management. *Organizational Dynamics*, 34, 77–87.

Leiter, M. P., & Maslach, C. (2005). *Banishing burnout: Six strategies for improving your relationship with work*. San Francisco, CA: Jossey-Bass.

Maslach, C., & Leiter, M. P. (1997). *The truth about burnout: How organizations cause personal stress and what to do about it*. San Francisco, CA: Jossey-Bass.

Maslach, C., & Leiter, M. P. (2000). *Preventing burnout and building engagement: Team member's workbook*. San Francisco, CA: Jossey-Bass, Inc.

Maslach, C., & Leiter, M. P. (2008). Early predictors of job burnout and engagement. *Journal of Applied Psychology*, 93(3), 498–512.

Schaufeli, W. B., & Salanova, M. (2014). Burnout, boredom, and engagement in the workplace. In M. C. W. Peeters, J. de Jong, & T. W. Taris (Eds.), *An introduction to contemporary work psychology* (pp. 293–320). New York: Wiley.

Sonnentag, S., Binnewies, C., & Mojza, E. J. (2010). Staying well and engaged when demands are high: The role psychological detachment. *Journal of Applied Psychology*, 95(5), 965–976.

Sonnentag, S., Mojza, E. J., Demerouti, E., & Bakker, A. (2012). Reciprocal relations between recovery and work engagement: The moderating role of job stressors. *Journal of Applied Psychology*, 97(4), 842–853.

Taylor, N. Z., & Millear, P. M. R. (2016). The contribution of mindfulness to predicting burnout in the workplace. *Personality and Individual Differences*, 89, 123–128. https://doi.org/10.1016/j.paid.2015.10.005

8

GETTING EVERYONE ON THE SAME PAGE

Cocreated program logic (COP)

Ulrica von Thiele Schwarz, Anne Richter, and Henna Hasson

Aim and justification for the cocreated program logic

In order to design, implement, and evaluate organizational interventions, theories of change are needed – that is, theories that outline why a certain intervention activity would be expected to have an effect on a specific distal outcome (Blamey & Mackenzie, 2007). Yet, overall, these types of theories are seldom used in organizational interventions (Biron & Karanika-Murray, 2013; Nielsen, 2013). This stands in contrast to the abundance of theories like the job demand resources (JDR) model and the effort reward imbalance model (e.g., Demerouti et al., 2001; Siegrist, 1996), which link exposure to factors in the work environment to employee health and well-being outcomes (Kristensen, 2005) and therefore may guide the content of an intervention. The idea of occupational health interventions is generally to improve employee health and well-being through an intervention that decreases exposure to demands and/or increases employees' resources. Thus, theories such as the JDR model are helpful in establishing the connection between change in job demands and resources and employee well-being. Yet, they are not helpful for linking the intervention to the change in job demands and resources. This is what theories of change are for.

Whereas efforts to develop and apply social, organizational, and psychological theories to illuminate how organizational intervention is brought about (e.g., Nielsen et al., 2014) are ongoing, the field of evaluation has a long tradition of using program logic for the same objective. Program logic, also known as program theory or logic models, outlines how an intervention, through its specific intervention activities, is related to a chain of outcomes, from the most proximal ones to more distal ones. This links the design and the implementation of an intervention to its evaluation, and thereby, makes the theory of change more explicit (Olsen et al., 2012; Rogers, 2008).

Program logic has often been constructed by interventionist (i.e., intervention developers such as consultants or researchers) (Saunders et al., 2005). Here, we propose a cocreation process involving multiple organizational stakeholders in addition to researchers and consultants. The program logic is then used as a guiding framework that runs through the creation of the intervention, its implementation, and evaluation. In the business field, the concept of cocreation was presented by Prahalad and Ramaswamy (2000), and has spread since. Cocreation is one of several terms (e.g., codesign, coproduction, cocare, etc.) stressing that design, implementation, and evaluation needs to be a joint venture of the researchers and the organization. Formally, cocreation is an interconnected, recursive set of interactions between stakeholders (e.g., managers, employees, researchers, and consultants; Payne et al., 2008; Prahalad & Ramaswamy, 2000). Instead of organizations being passive recipients of services and products ("value"), they are engaged in cocreating value, building on their unique perspective and knowledge (Payne et al., 2008). Thus, the cocreation process is a way to ensure that the intervention process is truly participatory.

A participatory approach is far from new in the context of organizational interventions; on the contrary, it is the recommended approach (Lamontagne et al.; Nielsen, 2013; Nielsen & Randall, 2012). It is well known that managers and employees are not passive recipients of an intervention, rather they are and should be actively engaged in shaping the intervention (Nielsen, 2013). Thus, an organizational intervention is not something researchers or consultants can design and implement, but something the organization and its members are, to varying degrees, active in designing and carrying out (McVicar et al., 2013; Nielsen & Miraglia, 2017).

In a participatory approach, actors with different kinds of knowledge, skills, and perspectives are welcomed to the table. In essence, this process ensures that the need to integrate theoretical and practical knowledge is met. The challenge, then, is to make sure the differences converge and that all stakeholders contribute to creating an intervention that will lead to the target outcomes and that provides the best possible match between the different knowledge sources. This includes what is known from research, as well as knowledge about the specific organization, from different sources within the organization. But how do you do this?

This chapter outlines a structured process – the cocreated program logic (COP) process – for how organizational stakeholders can be engaged in defining intervention goals and activities and thus forming the program logic together with interventionists (researchers or consultants). The program logic can then be used to guide the evaluation of the organizational intervention. In this chapter, will also present how COP can be used in two different ways: (1) to inform the evaluation of an intervention where the intervention activities are preset, and (2) to, in addition to informing the evaluation of the intervention, also design intervention activities. Three objectives form the background for this approach: the necessity of a cocreation process in participatory approaches, the need for program logic to guide the design, implementation, and evaluation of organizational interventions, and the need to link the two together in a structured way.

Cocreation to establish ownership and utilization of best available knowledge

As interventions have moved from focusing on changing individual health behaviors to target organizational and multilevel structures, the importance of engaging stakeholders across the organization has become evident. This engagement includes having employees and managers across the organization participate in change efforts to create a sense of ownership in the organization for the change process. In this sense, organizational interventions are less of a time-limited, externally induced project and more of an ongoing, continual improvement effort that is more closely linked to daily operations. As such, any organizational intervention needs to be aligned with organizational visions, goals, and objectives (i.e., vertical alignment) as well as fitting with daily operations (i.e., horizontal alignment; von Thiele Schwarz & Hasson, 2013). Thus, the intervention needs to provide a so-called philosophical fit (with the organization's vision and goals) and a practical fit (that is, be possible to do in consideration of possibilities and constraints in the organization; Moore et al., 2013).

The need for alignment and fit means that many stakeholders need to be involved in the design, implementation, and evaluation of organizational interventions. Stakeholders who bring unique perspectives and sources of knowledge about the organization include employees, line and senior managers, researchers, occupational health specialists, human resources specialists, change agents (e.g., employees with certain areas of responsibility such as safety champions), and/or consultants. *Employees* need to be involved since they are instrumental in bringing about change. *Line managers* are known to be able to make or break an intervention, but given their role in a hierarchical organization, they are in turn dependent on *senior managers*, who provide (or do not provide) recourses for line managers and employees (Hasson et al., 2014). They also bring a wider perspective on how an intervention relates to the overall strategies and objectives of the organization. Then there are specialists on the relationship between work factors and employee health outcomes, as well as specialists on change and evaluation. This can include people such as a *human resources specialists, consultants,* and *researchers.* Combined, these stakeholders bring theoretical and practical knowledge that is essential for making sure that each organizational interventions builds on the best available evidence from a wide range of sources (that is, not only research evidence). To achieve a unified and coordinated change effort, all these knowledge sources and perspectives need to be brought together in planning and designing interventions. This includes agreeing on the objectives for the intervention, as well as a joint understanding of which activities will most likely bring about the desired change.

Yet, few concrete suggestions and tools exist for how these kinds of processes can be realized in practice. For example, the interactions between researchers and the organization and its employees have not been particularly well defined in previous research – it may be everything from the organization or the employees simply accepting the intervention, to the organization and/or the employees having complete ownership of the change process (Kristensen, 2005). Similarly, participation may be direct or through representatives. The optimal level of participation is likely to differ between different organizations – one solution that fits to all organizations and interventions does not exist. For example, solutions may differ between interventions that the organization voluntarily commits to and interventions that are launched in response to external demands from changes in legislation or national guidelines, or between initiatives that comes from senior management and employee-driven changes. Thus, a tool is needed that is flexible enough to encompass different types of change processes, yet structured enough to provide a clear step-by-step guide for how participation throughout the design, implementation, and evaluation of organizational interventions can be achieved. Following this, the tool that we present is a suggestion on how a cocreation process can be set up and how it can look in practice.

Program logic: Outlining intervention components and target outcomes

The outcomes resulting from an organizational intervention generally develop as a chain of effects (Nielsen & Simonsen Abildgaard, 2013; von Thiele Schwarz et al., 2016) linking the components of the intervention to the outcome. For example, taking active part in an intervention (exposure and other implementation outcomes) aimed at redesigning how work is done (expressed in behavioral outcome) may lead to increased job autonomy and improved job clarity (intermediate outcome such as improved psychosocial work environment), which in turn increases job satisfaction and work engagement (distal outcomes such as employee well-being). That, in turn, may for example decrease turnover (end outcome such as organizational outcome). That is, each different outcome logically follows the previous one. This chain represents the program logic. It outlines the logic series of steps that are necessary for a chain of outcomes to be achieved.

The program logic, thus, outlines how the intervention is linked to the outcomes. This involves clarifying the core components of the intervention and the expected consequences of those components. Core components are the activities that are essential for the intervention to achieve its outcomes in that without them, the intervention will be less effective (or ineffective) (Fixsen et al., 2005). One can use multiple ways of outlining the core components. Outlines can be based on experience, previous empirical research of effective interventions, or theory. As described above, occupational health theories are helpful for guiding which and how outcomes (such as psychosocial work environment and employee health and well-being outcomes) are related; that is, the later stages of the program logic. For the earlier stages, other theories can be useful, including theories explaining behavioral change; for example, social learning theory and theory of planned behavior (e.g., Ajzen, 1991; Thomas et al., 2014) and theories explaining learning; that is, pedagogical theories such as constructive alignment (Biggs, 1996) and Vygotsky's zone of proximal development (Chaiklin, 2003).

By outlining how outcomes are expected to unfold, program logic also provides a framework for evaluation. As different effects follow on previous ones, this suggests *when* assessment of the different outcomes (i.e., *what* to assess) should be done in order to capture the effects. More so, the program logic can be viewed as an outline of the hypotheses for how the intervention will have its effect on outcomes. Having an a priori-specified model for the intervention is particularly important for organizational interventions that are not easily evaluated with randomized and controlled designs, and that aim to improve distal, multifactorial outcomes such as improvements in health (Kristensen, 2005). When outcomes are distal and multifactorial, it is difficult to link the changes or the lack of changes to the intervention. Thus, outlining and assessing more proximal, intermediate outcomes may allow the footprints of the intervention to be captured. In these circumstances, which are common for organizational interventions, the program logic provides an explicit and prospective way of studying the relationships between variables.

Getting everyone on the same page: Backward-moving program logic

Program logic can be developed in many different ways. Traditionally, the process involves starting with a predefined intervention where the core components are more or less known (e.g., stress management programs, mindfulness trainings, and leadership trainings). The intermediate and increasingly distal outcomes are then outlined in sequential order (Saunders et al., 2005). In contrast, the starting point in COP is at the outcomes: what goals are to be achieved? The logic is that in organizational interventions, achieving the outcome is more central than implementing a specific intervention. This approach is similar to that used in quality improvement research (Reed et al., 2014).

The backward-moving program logic is in line with the dynamic integrated evaluation model (DIEM; von Thiele Schwarz et al., 2016). This is an evaluation model for interventions that are dynamic (i.e., changing over time) and integrated (i.e., piggybacks on existing processes and structures in the organization) (von Thiele Schwarz et al., 2016). DIEM covers the intervention design, its implementation, further improvements of the intervention, and evaluation. The first four steps in DIEM cover the design phase, including decisions on objectives and target outcomes. COP can be used as a practical tool in these steps to define the intervention goals and intervention activities. After arriving at an intervention prototype (i.e., what activities we think are suitable), that is, the best current idea about how the intervention will look in the current context, the following DIEM-steps (five to eight) cover the implementation of the prototype and the potential revisions to it. These steps involve the continuous evaluation of how the intervention works in practice using data as a basis for potential revisions. Furthermore, evaluation involves the measurement of the intermediate and distal outcomes. COP is also a tool to define what type of outcomes should be measured and what are the optimal time points for these measurements. Thus, COP is central to several phases of an intervention.

Potential advantages of COP

Although it is possible for an interventionist or researcher to develop a program logic without involving other stakeholders, one of COP's defining features is that the program logic is cocreated amongst the group of stakeholders. This has a number of advantages.

First, cocreating the program logic may help get everyone on the same page, that is, to form a common understanding (a shared mental model) of the intervention (Nielsen & Randall, 2013). This decreases the risk of friction once the intervention is implemented. It may also decrease the risk of perceptual distance between stakeholders, that is, that different actors have different ideas and expectations about the intervention, its aim, goals, and needs (Hasson et al., 2016). As perceptual distance has been suggested to have a negative impact on the implementation of interventions as well as their outcome, decreasing perceptual distances concerning the intervention upfront may promote the successful implementation of the intervention (Hasson et al., 2016).

Second, cocreating the program logic may help build commitment and engagement. The necessity of having people across the organization on board is well known. By inviting those who will have opinions about the intervention, and allowing them to be able to influence whether it is implemented or not, a cocreated program logic means that those who can make or break the intervention will have invested time and intellectual capital in the development of it. This may increase the likelihood that they will assume ownership over the intervention as it unfolds.

Third, the program logic is likely to be more accurate if people with different knowledge sources and viewpoints have been involved in cocreating it. Having access to different knowledge sources (e.g., both theoretical knowledge about the intervention and practical knowledge about how things works in the organization) contributes to this.

Fourth, not only will the program logic be more feasible, the fit between the intervention and the setting where it is implemented is likely to be improved. The concept of intervention fit includes two interdependent dimensions: environment-intervention fit and person-intervention fit (Randall & Nielsen, 2012). By cocreating a program logic, constraints and opportunities in the organizational environment that may affect the intervention can be made explicit and managed by matching the intervention components to the needs in the organization, and (if needed) intervention components can be added aiming at managing obstacles for change. The cocreated program logic along with the adapted intervention can improve the perceived appropriateness of the intervention in the current environment (von Thiele Schwarz et al., 2016). Similarly, for those individuals involved and for those groups of employees they represent, person-intervention fit may be improved since the participants are likely to ensure that the intervention benefits them and those whom they represent. With a cocreation process with multiple stakeholders involved, this increases the chance that multiple viewpoints and needs will be addressed.

Lastly, by cocreating program logic the groundwork for the evaluability of the intervention is laid. The program logic forms a map that outlines what and when to evaluate and what data to collect. Since cocreating program logic helps establish a shared perception of the intervention activities and target outcomes as well as the mechanisms between them, those involved will understand the conclusions drawn from an evaluation, and thus, be more likely to embrace the findings (Blamey & Mackenzie, 2007; Leviton et al., 2010).

The COP process

The COP process builds on a structured methodology developed in higher education called adaptive reflection (Savage, 2011). Adaptive reflection combines the pedagogical theories of constructive alignment (Biggs, 1996), Bloom's taxonomy (Bloom et al., 1956) and Kolb's experiential learning process (Kolb, 1984). In constructive alignment applied in higher education, the outcomes that students are intended to learn are the starting point, and learning activities are aligned with these outcomes. It is important to note that the learning outcomes are expressed in active terms (e.g., describe, reflect, use, exemplify, etc.) that describe what performance is needed to achieve the outcomes. The active verb also indicates what kinds of learning activities are most suitable. For example, if the learning outcome is to apply something (e.g., give feedback), then the learning activity should provide opportunities to practice giving feedback. Bloom's taxonomy is a model covering a list of learning activities presented hierarchically, going from surface representations of learning (e.g., recognizing) through learning that reflects an increasingly greater ability to elaborate and use this knowledge (e.g., through describing, applying, analyzing, evaluating, and creating).

In the COP process, similar to adaptive reflection, the process of creating a constructive alignment between activities and outcomes is done with the stakeholders. They are led through a step-by-step process, outlined in Figure 2.1 (left-hand side). Figure 2.1 includes a description of the general steps as well as the ways the COP process was used in the two cases presented in this chapter, illustrating the flexibility of the tool.

The first step contains individual reflections over what it would look like if the outcomes of the intervention were achieved (see case descriptions for example). By reflecting individually at first, the benefits of having various perspectives is represented without risking anchoring effects and conformities, which regularly happen if one opinion is voiced before everyone has been able to contribute (Kahneman, 2011). Also, by asking the participants to build on their own experiences and then reflect and elaborate on them, the idea is to trigger a process of experiential learning (Kolb, 1984). The thoughts are documented on Post-it notes. In the second step, the Post-it notes are compiled and the participants asked to sort them into meaningful categories – initially under silence. This is, again, to allow individual interpretation, to avoid premature compromises, and to avoid the influence of power structures that may cap the knowledge becoming available in the group

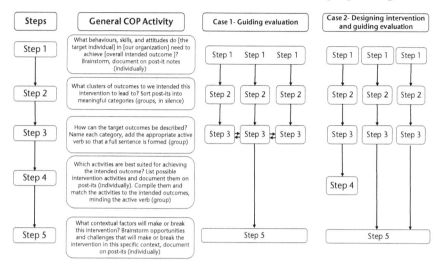

FIGURE 2.1   The COP process

(Savage, 2011). In the third step, each category is named and a suitable active verb is identified, forming a full sentence describing the target outcome in active terms. To help with this process, a list of active verbs can be presented (e.g., compare, analyze, inform, or reflect). In the fourth step, intervention activities are listed through individual brainstorming and then matched to the target outcomes. The final step in COP is to brainstorm factors that could make or break the intervention in this specific setting. This is also documented on Post-it notes individually.

Two cases of COP in action

In the following section, two cases illustrating how COP can be used in practice are described and discussed. First, a case where COP was used to create a common understanding of the objectives and to guide evaluation for a network-based learning model aiming to improve eHealth utility in a large health care organization is presented. The second case outlines how COP was used in a multilevel intervention including a first-line manager training intervention and a supporting senior management intervention (see also Chapter 9 for details on the senior management intervention). These cases are chosen to (a) outline how COP can be used to guide evaluation when the intervention is predefined (case 1) and (b) to inform the design of an intervention as well as guide its evaluation (case 2; see Figure 2.1, right-hand side). For each case, the contextual setting for the intervention and the background for the intervention are presented before explaining how COP was used. Then the results of the COP process are presented. We end each case by presenting some of the possibilities and limitations of using COP in the specific context of the case.

Case 1: Defining objectives to guide evaluation of an eHealth skills development intervention

Setting and background

This case focuses on a participatory employee skills development program. It was conducted in a regional health care organization in Stockholm County, Sweden, that included primary care, psychiatric care, habilitation, and rehabilitation divisions, as well as the five largest hospitals. The head of the primary care division, also responsible for the entire development program, contracted us in the autumn of 2015 to evaluate the intervention. The authors of this chapter had previously evaluated a similar intervention (Augustsson et al., 2017).

Intervention participants

All employees (i.e., 44,000 staff members) are expected to participate in the skills development program during 2017–2019. The intervention is a participatory skills development program consisting of a series of cross-professional workshops aimed to improve employees' skills in and use of information and communication technologies (ICT), clarify roles regarding ICT, decrease demands in general, increase work satisfaction, and also in a longer run strengthen employees' employability.

The intervention has a network design and is led by an internal *project management team* supported by *consultants* specialized in process evaluation. They work together with a group of *process instructors* to design the themes and materials for the workshops that form the content of the intervention. The process instructors are health care staff working in the organization and thus they are familiar with the organizational context. The process instructors' task is also to coach *development leaders*. These are employees who have volunteered to lead the workshops that are conducted at each unit. They are also expected to act as embedded change agents. Thus, the workshops are led by different development leaders across the different units, but they use the same structure, themes, and materials.

The participatory design of the workshops entails active participation of all employees in discussions, reflections, and practical exercises rather than didactic teaching. This also means that the questions discussed and the amount of time dedicated to different parts of a theme are allowed to differ somewhat between different sessions. Approximately 10 employees participate at each workshop session and every workshop theme is repeated until all employees in a unit have had the opportunity to participate. Overall the intervention includes three workshop themes. Each workshop lasts between 2.5 and 3 hours.

COP: Cocreated program logic to guide evaluation

In this case, COP was used to guide the intervention evaluation (agree on outcomes and the logic relationships between outcomes). This was done during one workshop in September 2016. Participants were process instructors (e.g., internal change agents, $n = 9$) and the project management team ($n = 3$). The focus was on explicating the outcomes of the development program for the three main groups in the network model: the employees, the development leaders, and the process instructors. The goal with the COP process was to facilitate the development of a shared understanding of the goals of the intervention. In particular, because the intervention was set up as a network model, the aim was to make clear the connections between actions and outcomes across the network. The defined outcomes then guided the intervention evaluation.

Rather than running the COP steps separately for each group (i.e., employees, developmental leaders, and the process instructors), we ran them in parallel during the same workshop as outlined below (see also Figure 2.1).

Step 1. Following the general COP process outlined above, the first step involved individual work. We tailored the process slightly by repeating the first step so that outcomes for each group (employees, development leaders, and process instructors) in the network were covered. First, all participants were asked to consider the outcomes for employees. The original COP question was "What behaviors, skills, and attitudes do employees need to have after the intervention so that the project goals are met?" This was tailored based on input from the participants so that it would reflect the participatory process of the intervention. Participants were therefore asked to think individually about the question "What behaviors do employees need to engage in when participating in the intervention so that the workshop goals and the overall project goals are met?" The participants wrote their thoughts on Post-it notes (one thought per note). The Post-it notes were compiled and put aside for the moment.

Next, step 1 was repeated focusing on development leaders, asking "What behaviors, skills, and attitudes do development leaders need to have for the project goals to be met?" Again, thoughts were written down on Post-it notes, which were compiled and separated from the employee notes. After this, the same procedure was repeated with focus on the outcome for the process instructors. At this stage, the question was "What additional behaviors, skills, and attitudes (than those already mentioned for development leaders) do the process instructors need to show for the project goals to be met?" The participants wrote their thoughts on Post-it notes, which were gathered and compiled separately from the two other levels' outcomes.

Step 2. Following the COP process, the Post-it notes were clustered within each group according to common themes. Now, the process for each of the actors in the network model (employees, developmental leaders, and process instructors) was run in parallel. The participants were divided into three groups. The participants worked in silence to sort the Post-it notes into themes.

Step 3. Once the groups were pleased with their themes, they were asked to discuss and to create headlines for the clusters. The clusters of Post-it notes for the developmental leaders dealt with the themes of being able to *collaborate and communicate* with all relevant stakeholders; having thorough *understanding* of people, the work conducted at the unit, ICT, and the organization; showing good *seminar leadership skills*; being able to *develop* in the role of seminar leaders; being able to *learn* from others; being able to *engage* all employees in the discussion (being able to listen, encourage those being more quite, being able to deal with those with strong emotions); and being *confident* in the participatory process, benefits of the training, and the organization being able to support them.

In an extension of step 3 of the original COP process, each group presented the headings to the rest of the participants. A discussion about the outcomes was facilitated by the researchers in order to create a common understanding of the headings and to get a deeper understanding of the themes.

The participants particularly highlighted that it became clear to them how the outcomes of the organization (on the employee level) were determined by how the developmental leaders were functioning, and how this, in turn, was dependent on how the process leaders acted. The groups also noted that the main themes were related to leadership and facilitation rather than content knowledge about eHealth. This was taken as an indication of the need to make sure this was reflected in the intervention activities for developmental leaders, which were initially focused more on eHealth content than change leadership. Due to the limited time that could be set aside for the workshop, this step did not involve finding active words as proposed in the original COP process.

Step 4. As this was an intervention where the intervention activities were already designed, the fourth step of listing intervention activities and matching them to the target outcomes was not applicable.

Step 5. The last step was an individual brainstorming activity to identify the organizational context that may influence the possibility of achieving the defined outcomes. The question the participants reflected upon was "What organizational context do development leaders need in order to succeed as seminar leaders?" Participants were instructed to think particularly about things that were feasible in their context, rather than visualizing the ideal organization where time and resources would be infinite. Again, thoughts were documented on Post-it notes. Aspects that were named was having mandate and support from their line manager and the process instructor were clear descriptions of what is expected of them, a general understanding in the organization that this participatory intervention is pri-oritized and linked to overall organizational objectives, feedback on performance from the project management team and the process instructors, capability to lead seminars and training in being able to do so, and practical aspects such as enough time allocated to the task as seminar leaders. This information was used to broaden the understanding among participants of the interconnectedness of the change ini-tiatives within the broader organizational context as well as to guide the evaluation (e.g., suggestions for possible mediators and moderators of change).

Finally, the information from the COP-workshops was used to inform the choice of measurement. Items of established scales were identified and mapped on the target outcomes to ensure that the evaluation reflected.

Lessons learned when COP is used to inform evaluation: A self-evaluation

In this case, COP was used to guide the evaluation of an eHealth development program, and we found that the process did so by providing valuable information. The clustering of outcomes showed which constructs needed to be included in the evaluation. The individual Post-it notes then helped ensure that the items reflected the specific meaning that the stakeholders attached to the construct. This can be thought of as a simple way of tailoring the measurement to the specific context, which has been suggested to be critical when evaluating organizational interventions (Nielsen et al., 2014). This grounds the evaluation in the context where it is conducted, increasing the likelihood that it will be meaningful for the organization and that it will be sensitive to the changes it aims to measure. In this case, the evaluation is still ongoing and thus, we do not yet have data on how the evaluation has been experienced so far; it has been helpful to be able to fall back on that content of the evaluation that was cocreated., helping to pave the way for acceptance of the results of evaluation, whatever they may be (e.g., evaluability; Leviton et al., 2010).

From observations of the workshop and the conversations that took place, it was clear that inviting organizational stakeholders engaged in the intervention to a joint workshop gave the group an opportunity to discuss the project goals in more concrete terms. It seemed to facilitate the development of a common understanding of the outcomes. This may be particularly important since the group included both the project management team and the process instructors, that is, those overall responsible for the intervention and those who had been asked to join so as to inform intervention activities and to facilitate the delivery of the intervention. Having a common understanding of the goals is crucial because the intervention builds on a network model where each instructor and seminar leader is supposed to use the same material and themes as a basis and thereafter allow certain variations in the actual execution of the participatory workshops. Being on the same page is likely to contribute to the different nodes of the network moving in the same direction.

Using outcomes on three levels for employees, development leaders and for process instructors, seemed valuable both for us as evaluators and for the organizational stakeholders. For us, it helped explicate the logic model linking activities in different parts of the network to the end (employee) outcome. By working through the outcomes for the different actors, the links between them became evident also for the participants in the workshop. For example, the participants noted that many more leadership-related tasks were involved in their picture of a successful developmental leader than, for example, ICT competences. In fact, some participants expressed a revelation about the fact that the role was much more of being a change agent than they had realized before. In addition, they were somewhat surprised to realize their own roles as process managers had an important function in forming a context that would give developmental leaders opportunities to lead, which in turn would be necessary in order for the outcomes on the employee level to be achieved. Overall, the importance of the process parts of the intervention, particularly the participatory approach, became clear through the COP process, suggesting that intervention activities targeting these areas may be needed.

Nevertheless, designing the intervention activities was beyond the scope of the evaluators' assignment as the intervention activities, overall, were preset. This is clearly a disadvantage, as relevant information became readily available through the workshop despite that the step specifically designed for this (step 4, Figure 2.1) was skipped. Therefore, even though the COP workshop gave input to the project management group, the usefulness of COP would have been even greater if the process also included informing the design of the intervention.

Working in parallel with the three different groups was a time-efficient way of covering a lot of material: the workshop only lasted 2 hours. It also saved the participants from the tedious repetition of going through the same process three times. Nevertheless, this may introduce a risk of developing different, rather than shared, understanding in the three groups. We tried to mitigate this risk by first having everyone contribute data for all three actors (step 1) before splitting into groups, and then, after the third step, letting the groups present and discuss each group's findings. Nevertheless, we would suggest adding another hour to the process to let this discussion take its time. This would also allow time to turn the headings of the clusters into meanings with active verbs, which was skipped because of time restraints. Adding that would allow more detailed analyses of the skills, knowledge, and behaviors than just description of the main themes.

Case 2: iLead – a multilevel intervention to foster implementation leadership

Setting and background

The second case focuses on a multilevel intervention that aimed to increase implementation leadership among line managers. This intervention was conducted in one division of the regional health care organization, with practices spread out throughout Stockholm County, Sweden. Senior management contacted us for help in the implementation of a working method that aims at facilitating and making care planning more effective. This implementation process had been on-going for approximately 18 months with a variety of setbacks.

Approximately 700 employees work in the division, which is divided into five thematic sections. Further, the sections are divided up into units, which are led by 33 line managers. The senior management group consists of nine members, who decided to invite all line managers to participate in the intervention. During the planning process, the senior management group also realized that they, too, needed to develop their own knowledge and skills about implementation and how to lead implementations, and thus, the line leadership intervention was complemented by a supporting intervention specifically for the senior management group.

Some of the content was similar, but overall, the senior management intervention focused on improving their ability to provide line managers with an optimal context to perform their implementation leadership. For further information about the project in general, see Richter et al. (2016), and for the senior management intervention in particular, see Chapter 9.

COP and intervention participants

Five national experts in implementation and leadership training (consults or researchers in the area) participated in the COP process preceding the intervention. Thirty-one line managers participated in the COP process and the intervention (one was unable due to ongoing organizational restructuring). The majority of participants were female, representing the general gender composition in health care. All participating managers chose a current implementation that was relevant for them to work on during the leadership intervention. In addition, the whole senior management group participated in the COP process and in the senior management intervention.

Using COP to design the intervention and guide evaluation

To design the intervention (the goals and the activities) and to guide the evaluation (agree on outcome and the causal relationships between outcomes), three separate COP workshops were conducted from winter 2015 to spring 2016.

The first COP workshop was conducted with experts. In addition to informing the design of the intervention and the evaluation in general, the specific goal was to get a coherent expert opinion about appropriate intended outcomes of implementation leadership training interventions and to identify intervention activities that where constructively aligned with those outcomes. Following the COP process outlined above, the followings steps were taken (see Figure 2.1, right-hand side).

Step 1. The experts were instructed to think individually about the question of "What behaviors, skills, and attitudes do managers need to lead an implementation?" They wrote down all thoughts on Post-it notes (one thought per note; see Table 2.1 for examples).

Step 2. The notes were compiled, and the experts worked together to sort them into meaningful categories, initially under silence.

Step 3. The experts then created headings for each cluster. These headings were iteratively revised until they contained an active verb, forming a full sentence that described an intended outcome of the intervention. To help with this process, the group was presented with a list of verbs. They were also asked to consider the level of proficiency that each verb represented in relation to knowledge, learning, and skills. In this way, the headings form the target outcomes for the line manager intervention (see Figure 2.2).

Step 4. To arrive at a list of intervention activities that matched the intended outcomes, the experts were asked two questions. First, they worked individually

FIGURE 2.2   The expert group in the process of matching intervention activities to the intended outcomes

FIGURE 2.3   The expert group reflecting on the identified the learning outcomes

generating answers to "Which activities have worked well in previous interventions?" The answers were documented on Post-it notes. These were compiled and the group jointly engaged in answering the second question: "Which of these learning activities would fit in the current intervention to achieve the target outcomes?" They matched the appropriate intervention activities to the intended outcomes (Figure 2.3). This included considering the verb (level of proficiency of knowledge and skill) and making sure the intervention activities were constructively aligned with the outcome. For example, the intervention outcomes "knowledge about relevant theoretical models" and "setting the implementation into a larger context" were intended outcomes that were identified by the experts. The ambition was also to include a variety of intervention activities such as how knowledge about the relevant theoretical models can be brought about (e.g., using short inspirational films, paper and pen exercises, etc.). See Table 2.1 for examples of identified intervention activities.

Step 5. Because the experts were not familiar with the specific context where this intervention would be implemented, this step was not applicable.

The *second* COP workshop targeted the 31 participating line managers. Their process involved steps 1–3 and 5.

Step 1. The first-line managers were asked to respond to the question "What behaviors, skills, and attitudes do managers in our organization need to lead an implementation?" Thus, they were asked to respond to a similar first question as the experts, but specifically considering leading implementation in their own organization. Similar to the experts, the line managers were instructed to generate as many Post-it notes as possible. See Table 2.1 for examples.

Step 2. Similar to the general COP process and that used in the expert group, the Post-it notes were compiled and then sorted into meaningful clusters, in silence. Because this was a larger group, this was done in groups of five to seven persons.

Step 3. Each smaller group was then asked to find headings for each cluster using active verbs. Compared to the expert group the line managers did not relate the active verbs to the level of proficiency that each verb represented. Here an adaptation was made to fit to time constraints for this workshop.

Step 5. Going directly to step 5, the managers were asked "What context/surrounding do line managers in our organization need in order to become good implementation leaders?" They were instructed to think particularly about things that were feasible in their organizational context, rather than visualizing the ideal organization where time and resources are infinite. Examples are presented in Table 2.1. For the sake of time, the line managers did not proceed with steps 2 and 3 for this question. Also, in contrast to the first question, which aimed at creating a common understanding of what implementation leadership is, the second aimed to provide input on what supporting activities would be needed, including informing the content of the senior management intervention. For example, it became evident that the managers needed clarity about the time frame for the implementation and that they longed for a more effective dialogue between senior and line managers.

TABLE 2.1 Examples from the different COP sessions

Experts	*Line managers*	*Senior management*
Question 1 What behaviors, skills, and attitudes do managers need to lead an implementation?	Question 1 What behaviors, skills, and attitudes do managers do managers in our organization need to lead an implementation?	Question 1 What behaviors, skills, and attitudes do first-line managers in our organization need to lead an implementation?
• Know about general leadership, in particular transformational leadership • Know about domain specific leadership • Know about implementation models • Know about behavioral change such as handling resistance • Communicate change in an understandable and meaningful way • Communicate the belief in employees' competence to handle the change • Be a role model • Be clear but flexible • Show support • Setting goals, monitor and give feedback	• Clear communication to employees • Understand the aim and purpose of the change • Understand the change process • Be knowledgeable • Prioritize and structure • Monitor and give feedback • Be open • Handle resistance • Motivate and inspire • Listen to employees • Set goals • Engage employees	• Lead the process • Express trust and loyalty • Know the implementation process • Know the content of the implementation • Stand behind the implementation • Create motivation • Communicate the implementation relating it to the greater goal of the organization • Be open and creative • Have a structure for the implementation • Be a role model • Monitor and give feedback
Questions 2 Which intervention activities have worked well in previous interventions?	Question 2 (spet 5) What context/surrounding do line managers in our organization need in order to become good implementation leaders?	—
Didactic tools:	• Recruitment of employees • Support for employees • Communication plan regarding the implementation • Support from the closest manager • Clear direction from senior management • Possibility to participate in decision making • Time plan • Prioritizing in the organization • Monitoring and feedback	—
• Video demonstration • World café		
Feedback and reflection:		
• Reflecting teams • Group discussion • Poster session		
Group work and role play Pedagogic models/theories		

Because steps 2–3 were done in smaller group, the line managers spent 5 minutes towards the end of the workshop looking at the headings and Post-it from the other groups. This was done to give them a sense of which themes the other groups had identified.

The third COP workshop was conducted with the senior management group. It followed the same steps as the process for line managers answering the question "What behaviors, skills, and attitudes do first-line managers in our organization need to lead an implementation?" They silently wrote down answers on Post-it notes, sharing the notes and sorting them in silence, then deciding on the heading for each cluster. Results of this workshop were similar to the results from the workshop with the line managers (see Table 2.1).

After the workshops, the senior management group and the line managers received a transcript of notes from their respective workshops. This was done as a memory aid and to give them input for further reflection. The senior management group also received transcripts from the first-line manager workshop.

Once the three workshops had been conducted, the next step involved creating a program logic. Here we added another source of information, namely scientific literature and theory on leadership and implementation and pedagogical principles. A scoping review on these topics was undertaken, particularly looking at the theoretical underpinnings, content, and pedagogical principles of published leadership interventions. The results from the COP workshops as well as from the literature review were mapped and outlined in a logic model. The researchers conducted this in an internal workshop (Figure 2.4). A brief overview of the program logic can be found in Table 2.2. Overall, the results from the COP process were well in line with the scientific literature and theory. The intervention activities identified by the expert group also largely overlapped with pedagogical approaches that have previously been used in leadership interventions.

The program logic was then used to guide the evaluation. This was done in an iterative fashion whereby items of established scales measuring constructs relevant to the intervention goals were mapped on the intended outcomes to ensure that the identified issues were covered in the evaluation. This process highlighted the need to develop a scale that specifically captured implementation-specific, full-range leadership (Mosson et al., forthcoming).

Lessons learned when COP is used design the intervention: A self-evaluation

In this second case, COP was used both to inform the design and the evaluation of the intervention using a series of COP workshops targeting different stakeholders (e.g., experts, line managers, and senior management). Overall, this approach seemed feasible to elicit the information needed to create a program logic that was contextualized to the organization. It also seemed a feasible way to foster a shared understanding of the goals of the intervention as well as the logical links

FIGURE 2.4 The researchers map the results from the COP process on theoretically and empirically derived concepts

TABLE 2.2 Brief version of the program logic

Core components	Immediate impacts	Short-term impacts	Distal outcomes
• Short lectures • Work with a practical case e.g. action plan & sustainability plan • Reflection in small groups and individually • Role-play • Feedback from employees, fellow participants • Try new leadership behaviors – work between the workshops • Booster email between the workshops	• Increased knowledge about implementation leadership and implementation models in general • Increased knowledge about the specific implementation process • Increased understanding about reactions to change, motivation • Increased self-efficacy to lead implementation • Improved ability to structure implementation	• Improved skills and capacity to handle resistance, listen to employees • More frequently express trust, communicate change in an understandable and meaningful way • Setting clear goals, monitor and give feedback more frequently • Create motivation to implement • Provide increased direction	• Increased implementation of the guidelines • Improved implementation climate • Improved work-related wellbeing • Improved productivity

between the content of the intervention and the objectives (target outcomes) of the intervention.

One of the advantages of using a series of workshops with the different stakeholders was that it allowed the COP process to include only the steps most relevant for each specific group. All did steps 1–3 answering the question of "What behaviors, skills, and attitudes do managers in our organization need to lead an implementation?" But the experts subsequently focused on intervention activities and linking them to outcomes, and line managers added information on contextual factors that could make or break the intervention.

The input from the experts (e.g., researchers and consultants) helped to ensure that all-important aspects (both practical and theoretical) in the design and evaluation of the leadership intervention were considered. Thus, this process allowed research and practice to be combined, incorporating multiple knowledge sources. As the experts had practical experience of working with complex interventions and leadership development, they were able to contribute with a practical perspective both in terms of what they felt managers needed to know and do and also of "what works" as intervention activities. By inviting experts working in different fields and using different learning approaches, a variation of perspectives was considered that might not have been included if only relying on literature reviews. Nevertheless, the expert group was a convenience sample of experts who were well known to the researchers, and the width of experience could have been even more diverse, for example, by including experts with other disciplinary backgrounds.

Whereas the experts' input helped incorporate the theory and practice of leadership development, the line managers helped contextualize the intervention by describing the influence of context. By doing so, they provided valuable information about what should be included in a supporting intervention, and it was essential for creating the content for the senior management intervention (Chapter 9; von Thiele Schwarz et al., 2016). The Post-it notes on the contextual challenges were categorized by the interventionists and a summary of the relevant categories was sent out before each senior management intervention workshop to increase the senior group's readiness for the workshop and purvey the sense of urgency of the topic.

Inviting line managers to the COP process had additional advantages. First, it was a way to get to know the participants and for them to get to know the researchers. Therefore, the workshop, which was the first contact with the line managers, was important to building a trusting relationship. Second, it was a way to build a common understanding amongst the line managers concerning what it meant to lead an implementation. It provided line managers with an opportunity to reflect on their work and role together with colleagues. They also received transcripts of the notes and headings from the smaller groups. The fact that the different groups had generated very similar topics further conveyed that the perceptions to a large degree were shared. Third, the workshop gave the managers the possibility to reflect upon their role as implementation leaders and mentally preparing them for the role they would be asked to take during the intervention. Although we lack data to support this claim at this point, we speculate that this may be a way to increase readiness for change.

This case also involved a separate COP process for senior management. For the researchers, this workshop was an important source of information, as it made explicit the expectations that senior management had on what the line managers needed to improve, which in turn made the expectations on the intervention and the interventionists explicit. Based on observations and comments from the senior managers during the workshop, the COP process also seemed to facilitate a better understanding of the complexity of implementation leadership. This provided a starting point to build on for the senior management intervention, as it clarified the demands the line managers were facing and how they can be assisted in their role as implementation leaders. Lastly, the COP process also meant that senior management got a sense of involvement and investment in the intervention. The COP process may be one way to increase the buy-in that is so important for the success of any organizational intervention.

The workshop with the senior management took 2 hours, but could very well have been expanded to also let senior management reflect on their own role in the change process. That would have been another source to shape the content of the supporting senior management intervention and should definitely be introduced if the senior management intervention is the primary rather than supporting intervention.

In this case, the different sources of information from the three stakeholder groups converged. This helped convey a sense of shared purpose that was particularly important given that the organization had experienced difficulties related to the implementation during the years preceding this intervention. It also made it seamless for the researchers to put the program logic together. Yet, there may not always be convergence between stakeholder groups. In these cases, the COP process will help illuminate any perceptual distance that may exist between different stakeholders. Such discrepancies will have to be managed, and to do so, it may be worthwhile to amend the COP process to also include more shared sense-making, similar to how it was done in the first case in this chapter.

The results from the COP process also largely converged with previous research and leadership theory. This could be interpreted as the process being superfluous but on the other hand, we believe this demonstrates the validity of the method (as well as the validity of the theories). From a research perspective, this means that we still could build the intervention on theory. Yet, we still received all the benefit of the cocreation process. Participants themselves had generated the content, likely increasing the sense of fit and relevance as well as ownership compared to a scenario in which the research team had presented a predefined solution to them. We believe that this can increase the person-intervention fit as well as the organization-intervention fit, which previously has been identified as a crucial factor to succeed with an intervention (Randall & Nielsen, 2012).

Conclusions

In this chapter, we present a structured process whereby organizational stakeholders and researchers are engaged in designing intervention activities and/or to inform the evaluation by outlining the objectives and outcomes, thereby cocreating a program logic. We illustrate it using two cases. The first shows how the COP process can be used to guide evaluation and support the development of a shared understanding among stakeholders for a predefined intervention. The second shows how COP can inform the design of the intervention, in addition to guiding evaluation. In both cases, we perceived the process to be immensely helpful to ensure a thorough work-through of the program logic as well as strengthen the collaborative relationships with the organization where the interventions were set.

The advantages of the current approach were as follows:

- The process provided a structured approach to integrating theory and practice. On the one hand, the process validated the relevance of theories linking participatory approaches and leadership to outcomes. On the other hand, it contextualized the theories, tailoring them to the needs of the organizations and describing them in the words of the participants.
- The process was flexible enough to allow changes to be made in response to needs expressed by participants (case 1). It also provided a sufficient balance between structure and flexibility to allow different stakeholder groups to focus on the steps most relevant for them (case 2).
- The process was active and engaging. The participants expressed that they enjoyed the workshops—they were perceived as engaging, fun, and thought provoking. They appreciated the practical approach rather than merely discussing issues. Thus, as a bonus, the positive experience helped increase positive expectations for the coming intervention.
- The COP process worked equally well with the different stakeholder groups—managers and change agents in multiple levels of the organizations. It also worked both for a predefined intervention and an intervention where the only the main form (a leadership training intervention) was predefined.
- Through the COP process, the stakeholders help delineate how the objectives of the organization could be achieved and what the target outcomes might be. In the discussions around the headings, the participants also touched upon the prioritization of outcomes and activities, which informed the researchers about the activities that were believed to have the greatest impact, to be most changeable, and to have the greatest possibility for positive spillover, issues that have been described as essential for matching an intervention to an organization (Michie et al., 2015).

Yet, based on our learning from the two cases, we propose two revisions to the COP process. These are summarized in Figure 2.5. The first is an addition of a sixth step. Similar to earlier in the COP process, this step involves clustering the

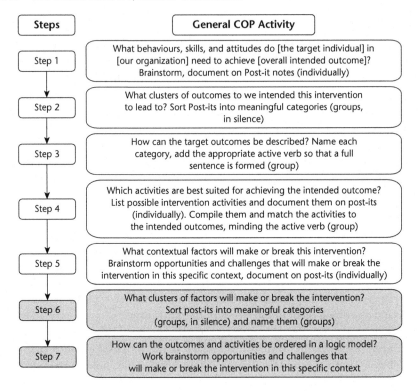

FIGURE 2.5   Revised version of the COP process

Post-it notes (from step 5) into meaningful categories and providing them with a heading. We believe this addition may help the group also develop a shared understanding about the context, further increasing the sense of being on the same page. The second revision is simply to explicate that the process also involves summarizing the findings in a program logic.

In addition, we recommend that the following is also considered:

- The time allowed for the process. In both cases, more than 2 hours would have been needed to allow more steps to be covered, and we would recommend others to allow at least 3 hours instead. Nevertheless, given the wealth of information earned on the current scale, the process does seem to be flexible enough to be valuable when time is more limited.
- Care is needed in the formulation of the questions. We have also used this process in the context of stress management and in that case, the question needed to focus less on skills, attitudes, and knowledge and more on an imagined positive end state (imaging that one wakes up tomorrow and one's work situation is in total balance: what would that look like?).

- In these cases, the researchers summarized the results from the COP process in a program logic, but this could also be done in collaboration with the organization. Yet, our experience is that people often perceive program logic to be a complex matter, and for the sake of using time and skills efficiently, it may be sufficient to have the interventionist summarize the information from the COP process in a logic model and then sense-checking it with the stakeholders.

References

Ajzen, I. (1991). The theory of planned behavior. *Theories of Cognitive Self-Regulation, 50*(2), 179–211.

Augustsson, H., Richter, A., Hasson, H., & von Thiele Schwarz, U. (2017). The need for dual openness to change: A longitudinal study evaluating the impact of openness to organizational change content and process on intervention outcomes. *The Journal of Applied Behavioral Science, 53*(3).

Biggs, J. (1996). Enhancing teaching through constructive alignment. *Higher Education, 32*, 347–354.

Biron, C., & Karanika-Murray, M. (2013). Process evaluation for organizational stress and well-being interventions: Implications for theory, method, and practice. *International Journal of Stress Management, 21*(1), 85–111.

Blamey, A., & Mackenzie, M. (2007). Theories of change and realistic evaluation peas in a pod or apples and oranges? *Evaluation, 13*(4), 439–455.

Bloom, B., Englehart, M., Furst, E., Hill, W., & Krathwohl, D. (1956). *Taxonomy of Educational Objectives: The classification of educational goals. Handbook I: Cognitive domain.* New York: David McKay Company.

Chaiklin, S. (2003). The zone of proximal development in Vygotsky's analysis of learning and instruction. In Kozulin, A., Gindis, B., Ageyev, V. & Miller, S. (Eds) *Vygotsk's Educational Theory and Practice in Cultural Context.* pp. 39–64. Cambridge: Cambridge University.

Demerouti, E., Bakker, A. B., Nachreiner, F., & Schaufeli, W. B. (2001). The job demands-resources model of burnout. *Journal of Applied Psychology, 86*(3), 499–512.

Fixsen, D. L., Naoom, S. F., Blase, K. A., Friedman, R. M., & Wallace, F. (2005). *Implementation Research: A Synthesis of the Literature.* Tampa: University of South Florida, Louis de la Parte Florida Mental Health Institute, The National Implementation Research Network (FMHI Publication #231).

Hasson, H., Villaume, K., von Thiele Schwarz, U., & Palm, K. (2014). Managing implementation: Roles of line managers, senior managers, and human resource professionals in an occupational health intervention. *Journal of Occupational* and *Environmental Medicine, 56*(1), 58–65.

Hasson, H., von Thiele Schwarz, U., Nielsen, K., & Tafvelin, S. (2016). Are we all in the same boat? The role of perceptual distance in organizational health interventions. *Stress and Health, 32*(4), 294–303.

Kahneman, D. (2011). *Thinking, Fast and Slow.* New York: Farrar, Straus and Giroux.

Kolb, D. A. (1984). *Experiential Learning: Experiences as the source of learning and development.* Englewood Cliffs: Prentice Hall.

Kristensen, T. (2005). Intervention studies in occupational epidemiology. *Occupational* and *Environmental Medicine, 62*(3), 205–210.

Lamontagne, A. D., Keegel, T., Louie, A. M., Ostry, A., & Landsbergis, P. A. (2007). A systematic review of the job-stress intervention evaluation literature, 1990–2005. *International Journal of Occupational* and *Environmental Health, 13*(3), 268–280.

Leviton, L. C., Khan, L. K., Rog, D., Dawkins, N., & Cotton, D. (2010). Evaluability assessment to improve public health policies, programs, and practices. *Annual Review of Public Health, 31*, 213–233.

McVicar, A., Munn-Giddings, C., & Seebohm, P. (2013). Workplace stress interventions using participatory action research designs. *International Journal of Workplace Health Management, 6*(1), 18–37.

Michie, S., Atkins, L., & West, R. (2015). *The Behaviour Change Wheel: A Guide To Designing Interventions.* London: Silverback Publishing.

Moore, J. E., Bumbarger, B. K., & Cooper, B. R. (2013). Examining adaptations of evidence-based programs in natural contexts. *The Journal of Primary Prevention, 34*(3), 147–161.

Mosson, R., von Thiele Schwarz, U., Hasson, H., Lundmark, R., & Richter, A. (forthcoming) How do iLead? Validation of a full-range leadership scale for implementation. Forthcoming.

Nielsen, K. (2013). Review article: How can we make organizational interventions work? Employees and line managers as actively crafting interventions. *Human Relations, 66*(8), 1029–1050.

Nielsen, K., & Miraglia, M. (2017). What works for whom in which circumstances? On the need to move beyond the "what works?" question in organizational intervention research. *Human Relations, 70*(1), 40–62.

Nielsen, K., & Randall, R. (2012). The importance of employee participation and perceptions of changes in procedures in a teamworking intervention. *Work & Stress, 26*(2), 91–111.

Nielsen, K., & Randall, R. (2013). Opening the black box: Presenting a model for evaluating organizational-level interventions. *European Journal of Work and Organizational Psychology, 22*(5), 601–617.

Nielsen, K., & Simonsen Abildgaard, J. (2013). Organizational interventions: A research-based framework for the evaluation of both process and effects. *Work & Stress, 27*(3), 278–297.

Nielsen, K., Simonsen Abildgaard, J., & Daniels, K. (2014). Putting context into organizational intervention design: Using tailored questionnaires to measure initiatives for worker well-being. *Human Relations, 67*(12), 1537–1560.

Olsen, K., Legg, S., & Hasle, P. (2012). How to use programme theory to evaluate the effectiveness of schemes designed to improve the work environment in small businesses. *Work: A Journal of Prevention, Assessment and Rehabilitation, 41*, 5999–6006.

Payne, A. F., Storbacka, K., & Frow, P. (2008). Managing the co-creation of value. *Journal of the academy of Marketing Science, 36*(1), 83–96.

Prahalad, C. K., & Ramaswamy, V. (2000). Co-opting customer competence. *Harvard Business Review, 78*(1), 79–90.

Randall, R., & Nielsen, K. (2012). Does the intervention fit? An explanatory model of intervention success and failure in complex organizational environments. In C. Biron, M. Karanika-Murray, & C. Cooper (Eds) *Improving Organizational Interventions for Stress and Well-being. Addressing process and context.* pp. 120–134. New York and London: Routledge.

Reed, J. E., McNicholas, C., Woodcock, T., Issen, L., & Bell, D. (2014). Designing quality improvement initiatives: the action effect method, a structured approach to identifying and articulating programme theory. *BMJ Quality & Safety, 23*(12), 1040–1048.

Richter, A., von Thiele Schwarz, U., Lornudd, C., Lundmark, R., Mosson, R., & Hasson, H. (2016). iLead –a transformational leadership intervention to train healthcare managers' implementation leadership. *Implementation Science*, *11*(1), 108.

Rogers, P. J. (2008). Using programme theory to evaluate complicated and complex aspects of interventions. *Evaluation*, *14*(1), 29–48.

Saunders, R. P., Evans, M. H., & Joshi, P. (2005). Developing a process-evaluation plan for assessing health promotion program implementation: A how-to guide. *Health Promotion Practice*, *6*(2), 134–147.

Savage, C. (2011). Overcoming Inertia in Medical Education. Doctoral thesis, Karolinska Insitutet, Stockholm.

Siegrist, J. (1996). Adverse health effects of high-effort/low-reward conditions. *Journal of Occupational Health Psychology*, *1*(1), 27–41.

Thomas, A., Menon, A., Boruff, J., Rodriguez, A. M., & Ahmed, S. (2014). Applications of social constructivist learning theories in knowledge translation for healthcare professionals: A scoping review. *Implementation Science*, *9*(1), 1.

von Thiele Schwarz, U., & Hasson, H. (2013). Alignment for achieving a healthy organization. In G. F. Bauer & G. J. Jenny (Eds) *Salutogenic Organizations and Change*. pp. 107–125. Dordecht: Springer.

von Thiele Schwarz, U., Lundmark, R., & Hasson, H. (2016). The dynamic integrated evaluation model (DIEM): achieving sustainability in organizational intervention through a participatory evaluation approach. *Stress and Health*, *32*(4), 285–293.

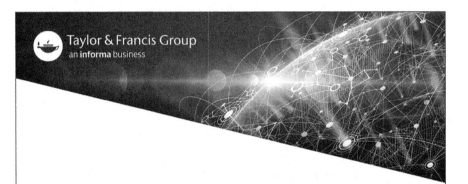

Printed in the United States
By Bookmasters